D0942220

APPETIZERS IN A JAPANESE MOOD

APPETIZERS
IN A JAPANESE MOOD

The Joy of Adding Japanese Dishes to your Menus

Yukiko and Robert Haydock
Introduction by Alice Waters

KODANSHA INTERNATIONAL
Tokyo • New York • London

Thanks:
To Gump's, 250 Post Street, San Francisco, California
94108, for providing all of the western and many of the
Japanese plates and dishes for the photography.

Distributed in the United States by Kodansha America, Inc.,
114 Fifth Avenue, New York, N.Y. 10011, and in the United
Kingdom and continental Europe by Kodansha Europe Ltd.,
Gillingham House, 38-44 Gillingham Street, London SW1V
1HU. Published by Kodansha International Ltd., 17-14 Otowa
1-chome, Bunkyo-ku, Tokyo 112, and Kodansha America, Inc.

Copyright © 1984 by Kodansha International Ltd.
All rights reserved. Printed in Japan.
                                    LCC 84-80163
                              ISBN 4-7700-1653-0

First edition, 1984
First paperback edition, 1992
92   93   94   5   4   3   2   1

CONTENTS

Introduction

I have always been fascinated by Japanese food. I like those tastes—the salty hot condiments . . . the fish so fresh it is often eaten raw . . . the vegetables so perfectly and lightly fried, or steamed, or grilled . . . the wonderful courses devoted to vegetables only—I like that the dishes are all served with a simplicity that permits us to taste the flavors and experience the textures of the wonderful ingredients. And it is not only the way it tastes, but the combination of the way it looks and tastes and how it is served that attracts me as a cook and restaurant owner (and as an eater!) to Japanese cuisine. And what appeals to me about FOOD IN A JAPANESE MOOD is the idea of adapting Japanese dishes for American cooks and making them accessible in light of our menus. The photos show just how enticing these dishes can be.

The refinement of the Japanese culinary aesthetic is really quite extraordinary. Japanese society is state-of-the-art, up-to-the-minute and is at the same time deeply tied to its cultural history and traditions. This contrast—the joining of old and new—is naturally reflected in the cuisine, which in exploiting today's harvest, calls upon a highly developed aesthetic tradition.

In 1983 I had the singular opportunity to visit Japan with Cecilia Chiang, who is a very fine cook and who once owned a restaurant in Tokyo. She took me around all of the little back streets, where we found people cooking and serving simply grilled brochettes of every description—tiny green peppers . . . ginkgo nuts . . . chicken livers and hearts . . . *shiitake* mushrooms . . . and I imagined any and all of them as perfect hors d'oeuvres at Chez Panisse.

In Kyoto we went to a sushi bar that catered principally to local people—nobody spoke English nor was any fish displayed in the usual countertop manner. The fish we ordered was taken from the tank in which it was swimming and filleted on the spot and the meat sliced to be eaten raw. Its bones were deep fried and served deliciously crunchy. Elsewhere we ordered beef, and watched and smelled it being grilled right before us. This immediacy—fish from the water to the table . . . foods cooked before your eyes—is just essential if we want to preserve the real and healthy tastes and textures of food, and is always evident in the best of Japanese cooking. The ingredients are right there—nothing is hidden.

The size of Japanese portions is something I find very inviting. I've realized that I easily lose my appetite when confronted with a large mound of food. I have often asked my waiter for another dish so that I can serve myself a smaller quantity. I've always thought that each course in a meal would be most appealing and enjoyable if it were small and tangy . . . that each course should pique the palate and draw you toward the next, rather than satiating you by sheer force of quantity. I have often cooked dinners at home that consist of many savory little dishes, and skip the "entree" entirely. My favorite and most memorable Japanese dinners have been just that—*kaiseki* tea ceremonies—where I've been served dish after dish of beautiful, tasty little foods.

I believe it is finally the freshness of ingredients that makes a dish truly enticing. I've become so devoted to freshness that for my restaurant we have sought to grow and raise our own ingredients so they can be gathered on the day we serve them, just hours before they are eaten. I have a passion for the shimmering and shiny just-opened oyster . . . a just-picked flower on a sushi plate . . . ice cream eaten right off the dasher. A friend of mine who shares this passion foregoes the use of refrigeration in his New Orleans restaurant, despite that warm climate, and plans his purchases so that all his foodstuffs are cooked and served on the day they arrive in his kitchen.

A most difficult but critical challenge for a cook is to respect the seasons—to be flexible enough to adjust the menu to what is available. You do a different kind of planning, because the ingredients may not turn out to be what you had expected. In our country you get the mistaken impression that everything is available all of the time. Yes, we can buy tomatoes in February, but they don't taste like tomatoes, and they cost a lot more than they do in September. We have fruits imported from foreign lands, but they aren't as good as those picked ripe and eaten at once. After twelve years of restaurant cooking I've learned to resist buying asparagus until the first local spring asparagus comes up. There is an enormous pleasure that comes with the waiting . . . the anticipating. The whole focus of Japanese food is seasonal—the dishes change to accord with the change of ingredients—and the result is a cuisine with both presence and vitality.

As cooks in a relatively young country, we are on an exciting path of discovery—we are just learning what foods are available to us locally, and about how they taste . . . and look . . . and smell . . . and combine—we are still experimenting and searching. Along the way, we've recognized more and more an affinity with the Japanese approach to foods, and we've found that Japanese cuisine offers a wealth of lessons and wisdom about the integrity of our foods and about the appeal and aesthetics of their presentation.

Alice Waters

Preface

Westerners in greater numbers than ever before are becoming familiar with Japanese cuisine. Discovering it is like encountering a culinary Shangri-la, rich, perfected, but seemingly private and mysterious. This book has been written to help dissolve some of the mystery. The discoveries you make will be worth the journey.

Almost four and one-half centuries ago, three shipwrecked Portuguese traders made a historic landfall on Tanegashima Island, in the rough Pacific waters off the southern coast of Kyushu. This was the first recorded contact between any western peoples and the Japanese on Japanese soil. Undoubtedly the famished seamen became instant enthusiasts for everything the island offered, especially food and water. Once revived however, the strange Japanese diet probably paled, leaving them longing for a crackling Portuguese roast pig and a flagon of wine.

The intervening centuries have not seen much change in western understanding or acceptance of Japanese food. In America, our cattleman's heritage still lingers on. We are a meat-and-potatoes people. And may always be. But recently, changes have been occurring in our eating habits—or if not in our habits, at least in our eating interests—which were unforeseen a decade ago. Important numbers of people are seriously concerned over the nutritional problems of the high-fat diet. Nutritional concerns have even penetrated the culinary bastions of haute cuisine, with the result that the traditional French chef's pride—the rich, butter-laden sauce—is no longer welcome.

But health worries by themselves can't account for the enormous enthusiasm for Japanese cuisine. What does account for it is the simple discovery that it tastes wonderful.

It is unlikely that there exists anywhere in the world of culinary writing a more affectionate tribute to the freshly gathered, freshly shelled green pea than the four delicious pages M.F.K. Fisher has given us in her *Alphabet for Gourmets*. She has described the "unbelievable summit of perfection" that can be reached when the path from the garden to the table is short and loving. The Japanese share this love affair with fresh, seasonal food. If it is not in season, it is simply not available in many Japanese restaurants. Living with life's natural scarcity means we can fully enjoy nature's treasures when she serves them up. They say that eating a food that is just coming into season will add seventy-five days to your life. This book is dedicated to all those extra days.

A WORD ABOUT THE BOOK

It was planned with two objectives in mind. First, to take you foraging around in the wonderland of Japanese food. This in itself should be a lot of fun. The second objective is more specific. Dishes have been chosen that work well as part of a western menu, as either a light luncheon course, or a side dish, or a delightful first course to excite you for the wonderful things to come.

The book has been done in a very visual style. It is hoped that the photographs and drawings help to make these dishes a little more accessible. We apologize for those times that you find it oversimplified, and regret those times when we haven't simplified enough. We hope, on balance, that it is a book you can work with. The cuisine deserves it.

Finally, thanks are in order. First to our friend Alice Waters for happily agreeing to do the introduction in spite of the unremitting demands of a new restaurant opening, an imminent trip to Italy, and, most demanding of all—a new baby girl.

Thanks also to our friends at Gumps—Marilu Klar, Richard Singer, Rachel Brinkley, and Vera Anderson, who generously let us browse among the beautiful things to select tableware for the photographs.

Our thanks especially go out to Katsuhiko Sakiyama of Kodansha International in Tokyo, who has shown the great Japanese quality of patience in carefully guiding the book to completion in spite of our sometimes meandering path. And to our editor, Michiko Hiraoka, who in the nicest possible way has simply demanded the best. We have failed her in that, but the book is much better than it would have been without her.

And finally to the generations of Japanese chefs who have patiently and faithfully developed their cuisine, and whose knowledge and skill we have only partially been able to convey to you.

YH & RH
Mill Valley
May 1984

Ingredients

AGAR-AGAR (kanten): In Japan, aspics are made with this gelatin derived from seaweed (Western gelatin is derived from animal bone). For this reason, agar-agar is often available in healthfood stores. The Japanese product comes in 1-inch-square bars about 10 inches long; this is the form being used in this book. It is also available in powder, stick, flake, and pellet form.

Agar-agar has the great advantage of setting at a much higher temperature than Western gelatin. Thus it does not soften or get runny at room temperature. Further, it has a much more delicate texture than bone gelatin and is not as rubbery.

ARROWROOT: Arrowroot is a fine white powder consisting of about 80 percent starch obtained from the roots of various tropical rhizomes. It is being used in this book in place of cornstarch as a thickener because it has superior clarity and has no taste of its own. It is readily available on supermarket spice racks. Japanese *kuzu* (*kudzu*) starch is often mistakenly referred to as arrowroot. It is an extremely high-quality, expensive thickener made from the root of the *kuzu* plant.

BONITO FLAKES, DRIED
***kezuri-bushi* or *hana-katsuo*:** Packaged thinly shaved dried bonito flakes. This form is to be distinguished from *katsuo-bushi*, which is the dried bonito fillet itself. The latter is shaved in the kitchen with a plane-like device immediately prior to use. Naturally, the flavor of freshly shaved flakes is superior, but packaged bonito flakes are acceptable and used universally throughout Japan. When choosing *kezuri-bushi*, select flakes with a pinkish color. The name *hana-katsuo* ("flower bonito") derives from the fact that the pinkish

shavings are the finest quality, and the color is reminiscent of cherry blossoms. Store in an airtight container in the freezer.

***ito-kezuri*:** This is dried bonito shaved into thread form, as compared to the conventional bonito flakes used to make *dashi*. It is used for garnishing as well as dressing foods. It imparts a unique sealike flavor, which is apparent even after frying. If *ito-kezuri* is not available, the conventional flakes may be substituted, but they should be rubbed between the palms of your hands to give them a threadlike form. Store in an airtight container in the freezer.

DAIKON: This giant radish is most familiar to Americans in its large, tubular shape, often growing to a foot or more in length and four to five inches in thickness. In Japan it is grown in numerous sizes and shapes. Although daikon is available throughout the year, the autumn to winter months bring the most delicious, succulent crops. Daikon is also prized for its healthful properties. It contains high quantities of vitamin C as well as enzymes to aid digestion. This is probably the reason that grated daikon is always added to dipping sauces used for tempura and as an accompaniment for oily fish. Daikon becomes aromatic and hot immediately upon grating; the flavor remains lively for 7 or 8 minutes, becoming quite bland after about an hour.

DAIKON SPROUTS: These sprouts can be grown at home. The seeds are readily available in healthfood stores. They grow about 4–5 inches long, and, unlike alfalfa, the stems are nice and straight. They make a very attractive garnish.

***DASHI*:** This is the stock made from dried bonito flakes and kelp. See page 155.

DOMYOJI-KO: *Domyoji-ko* is glutinous rice that has been dried and granulated. It is used in confections and as a coating in deep-frying. See page 155 for a homemade version.

EGGPLANT (JAPANESE): Eggplant is another vegetable that nature packages in many sizes, shapes and colors. Eggplants vary from the size of a chickpea to as much as 8 inches in length and 5 inches in diameter; shapes vary from globular to long and tubular. They can be pure white, green, pale or dark purple or striped. The small 4-5 inch dark purple variety is most familiar in Japan. The Japanese eggplants are more delicate and less watery than the large, egg-shaped American varieties. Try to choose the youngest and tenderest eggplants if the smaller Japanese variety is not available.

ENGLISH CUCUMBER: Most cucumbers have a tough skin and large seeds. The English cucumber is meaty, seedless, and has tender, thin skin. The ideal size is $1\frac{1}{2}$ by 12 inches, although it can grow to 24 inches long. They are not expensive and are carried by many markets.

ENOKI MUSHROOMS (enokidake): These strange little mushrooms are just beginning to find their way into American markets and are also known as snowpuff mushrooms. They are small, white, and slender. The stem is about 5 inches long and quite thin, culminating in a small button cap.

GINGER, FRESH: Be certain to always use fresh ginger root—never the dried or powdered form. This knobby root is available in most supermarkets. When wrapped in plastic it can be successfully refrigerated for about two weeks.

GINGER JUICE: Ginger juice is obtained by squeezing a piece of fresh ginger in a garlic press or by finely grating fresh ginger and squeezing out the juice in cheesecloth or with your fingers.

GINGER, PICKLED: There are primarily two kinds of pickled ginger. *Hajikami* is pickled in rice vinegar and sugar and is a delicate pink in color. It has a sweet/sour flavor. *Beni shoga* is pickled in salt and vinegar and dyed a bright red. It has a tart, salty taste. Both come sliced, julienned, or in chunk form.

GINKGO NUTS: The ginkgo tree comes in male and female gender. The female bears the green fruit (ginkgo nut). The white shell is soft and easy to crack and remove. The nuts should then be blanched in hot water, which makes the thin brown inner skin easier to peel away.

GOURD RIBBONS (kampyo): A type of calabash gourd is shaved and the strips are dried in the sun. Choose thick, wide strips that are creamy white in color. Milky white ones should be avoided, since they may have been bleached. Yellow, shriveled ones are of poor quality or too old.

HARUSAME: These filaments are made from potato starch. The Japanese name translates as "spring rain," which derives from their slender, translucent quality. Unlike it's cousin, made from mung beans, *harusame* disintegrates if cooked in liquid too long. When used in soup, it should be added at the last minute. When fried, it puffs up instantly to snowy white.

KELP, KONBU: *Konbu* is giant kelp, which is harvested primarily from the cold seas of the island of Hokkaido. It is one of the two main ingredients in *dashi*, the important Japanese cooking stock.

KONBU DASHI: This vegetarian form of *dashi* is made without bonito. Simply soak *konbu* kelp in water for several hours. See page 155.

LOTUS ROOT (renkon): This tubular rhizome grows in links like a sausage about 5-7 inches in length and about $2\frac{1}{2}$ inches thick. It is distinguished by its crunchy white flesh, which contains tubular hollows that run the length of each link.

MATSUTAKE MUSHROOMS: *Matsutake* is a highly prized Japanese mushroom. It cannot be cultivated and so must be hunted in red pine forests. In the western United States, the mushroom makes its appearance in September and lasts through November. Many West Coast *matsutake* are shipped to Japan. It is a large mushroom with a thick, often short stem. Select unopened or slightly open caps with firm stems.

MIRIN (sweet cooking saké): Mixtures of steamed glutinous rice, rice malt, and saké are set to ferment for 2-3 months. The result is *mirin*, a sweet cooking saké with an alcohol content of about 13 percent.

MISO: This fermented soybean paste is becoming quite well known in the West. It is simply not possible to list all of the ways that *miso* is used. It is enough to say that it is one of the distinctive tastes of the orient and is destined for greater and greater impact in western kitchens as familiarity grows. Broadly speaking, there are three types—white, red, and dark.

NORI SEAWEED: *Nori* is cultivated tangle; it comes packaged in dried thin, blackish sheets measuring about 6×8 inches. Americans know it as the wrapping for many varieties of sushi. *Nori* is best stored in an airtight container, kept in a cool dry place. It may also be wrapped well in foil and frozen.

PAK-CHOI (often spelled "bok choy"): This small, tender Chinese green is used in this book as a substitute for *komatsuna*, a leafy green that is abundant in Japan but not available in North America.

PICKLED PLUMS (umeboshi): These are small, intensely salty, pickled plums. Red *shiso* (perilla) leaves are included in the pickling process to impart flavor and the distinctive reddish color. *Umeboshi* probably require some getting used to; but they are considered to be a very healthy food with great benefits for the digestion and intestinal tract. They are usually available in healthfood stores, and certainly in oriental markets.

RICE VINEGAR: A vinegar made from naturally fermented rice. It is milder than the familiar western vinegars.

SANSHO POWDER: The tangy seeds of the *sansho* tree, which are about the size of peppercorns, are ground to produce *sansho* powder—a popular Japanese seasoning.

SAKÉ: In addition to its well-known qualities as a beverage, saké is one of the main flavoring ingredients in Japanese cuisine. It contains about 19 percent alcohol. Japanese chefs sometimes simmer saké before using to eliminate the alcohol. It is available in most U.S. liquor stores.

SEA URCHIN (uni): *Uni* is the Japanese word for sea urchin as well as sea urchin roe. The fresh roe comes neatly packed in a single layer in small wooden trays. It can also be purchased cooked, seasoned, and preserved in a jar (*neri uni*). Once the jar is opened, it should be refrigerated and used rather quickly. *Neri uni* is delicious spread on toast as an appetizer.

SESAME SEEDS: Sesame seeds are widely used in Japanese cooking for their fragrance and flavor. Both black and white sesame seeds are available. The choice usually depends on the color accent desired rather than on flavor. The seeds are always toasted lightly before using to release their flavor and aroma. They may also be ground for sauces and dressings. It is easy to overtoast them, however, and difficult to say how not to. The skilled chef "just knows" with that culinary sixth sense that signals when things are right. In general, toasting should take about a minute in a dry pan over medium heat. The seeds should be shaken and stirred constantly. Remove from heat as soon as seeds begin to make popping sounds. If you are going to grind them, do so immediately in a mortar or *suribachi* (Japanese grinding bowl), while seeds are hot.

SESAME SEED OIL: This is an expensive, nutty flavored oil made from sesame seeds. It is primarily used for flavoring and not for cooking. But if your palate demands the best, it will produce the definitive tempura. Tempura made with sesame oil will even taste delicious the next day, assuming there are any leftovers. Chinese sesame seed oil should be avoided, since it often has a bitter taste.

SHIITAKE MUSHROOMS: *Shiitake* mushrooms are currently being cultivated in California. They are grown on the bark of the *shii* tree and other species related to the oak. They may be purchased either fresh or dried. The dried mushroom has a more intense flavor. Select ones with thick, rounded caps, preferably with cracks in them. These are more costly but of high quality.

SOBA (BUCKWHEAT) NOODLES: *Soba* noodles are made from a mixture of buckwheat flour and wheat flour. They are distinguished by their brownish-gray color. Available in healthfood stores.

SOMEN (FINE WHEAT) NOODLES: *Somen* noodles are very thin, white wheat noodles, often eaten cold on hot summer days. Sometimes used as garnish in clear soup.

SOY SAUCE: This well-known salty brown sauce is made from fermented soybeans, wheat, and salt. It comes in both light and dark varieties—the light variety is saltier than the dark and is used to avoid darkening the color of foods, not for flavor reasons. A mild variety is also produced that has a lower salt content (8.8 percent).

TAMARI: Tamari is made from soybeans and looks like thick soy sauce. Some feel that its flavor is superior to soy sauce. Many restaurants in Japan use it with sashimi.

TOFU: Japan extracts three important products from the soybean—*miso*, soy sauce, and tofu. To create tofu, soy milk is coagulated into curd, which is poured into molds. Smaller cakes are cut from these blocks. Tofu is marketed in the U.S. packed in water in small, sealed, date-stamped plastic tubs. Tofu should always be kept floating in water and refrigerated. The water should be changed daily.

TREFOIL (*mitsuba*): This cultivated parsley-like herb has a distinguishing triple-leaf structure and a bright, light green color. It closely resembles cilantro in form and color, but is far milder and gentler in flavor. It is carried in some oriental groceries. Seeds are also available, and the plant is easily grown in a damp, shady place.

WASABI: Sometimes known as Japanese horseradish, the *wasabi* plant grows in cold, clear mountain streams. The root is grated and used with sashimi and sushi. Powdered *wasabi* is available in oriental foodstores, packaged in small tins. Shortly before serving, a teaspoon or two of the powder is mixed vigorously (usually with the end of a chopstick) in a small cup with enough cold water to form a stiff paste. The *wasabi* paste is kept covered until serving time.

WINTER MELON: This Chinese vegetable is a large green-skinned melon with flavorless flesh. It enhances other flavors and is enjoyed for its texture.

Measures, Temperatures, and Weights

Liquid Measures

ounces × 29.57 = milliliters (mL)
milliliters × 0.034 = ounces
quarts and liters are almost the same:
quarts × 0.95 = liters (L)
liters × 1.057 = quarts

CUPS, PINTS, QUARTS	SPOONS 1 tsp = 5 mL 1 Tbsp = 15 mL	FLUID OUNCES	MILLILITERS
¼ cup	4 Tbsps	2 oz	59 mL
⅓ cup	5 Tbsps + 1 tsp	2⅔ oz	79 mL
½ cup	8 Tbsps	4 oz	118 mL (120 mL)
⅔ cup	11 Tbsps − 1 tsp	5⅓ oz	157 mL
¾ cup	12 Tbsps	6 oz	177 mL
1 cup	16 Tbsps	8 oz	236 mL
2 cups (1 pt)		16 oz	473 mL
4 cups (1 qt)		32 oz	946 mL (1 L)

1 American cup = 240 (236) mL = 8 American fl oz

Temperatures

$$\text{Fahrenheit} = \frac{\text{Celsius} \times 9}{5} + 32$$

$$\text{Celsius} = \frac{(\text{Fahrenheit} - 32) \times 5}{9}$$

DEEP-FRYING OIL TEMPERATURES

300°F/150°C—330°F/165°C=low
340°F/170°C—350°F/175°C=medium
350°F/175°C—360°F/180°C=high

Weights

ounces×28.35=grams
grams×0.035=ounces

POUNDS	OUNCES	GRAMS
	1 oz	30 g
	2 oz	60 g
	3 oz	85 g
¼ lb	4 oz	115 g
½ lb	8 oz	225 g
¾ lb	12 oz	340 g
1 lb	13 oz	450 g

Linear Measures

inches×2.54=centimeters
centimeters×.39=inches

INCHES	CENTIMETERS
⅛ in	½ cm
¼ in	¾ cm
⅓ in	⅘ cm
⅜ in	1 cm
½ in	1½ cm
¾ in	2 cm
1 in	2½ cm
1½ in	4 cm
2 in	5 cm
2½ in	6½ cm
3 in	8 cm
4 in	10 cm

VINEGARED AND DRESSED DISHES

1. Prawns in Golden Cloaks (page 34)

2. Chicken Nest (page 36)

3. Icicle Oysters (page 39)

4. Enoki Mushroom Salad with
Salmon Caviar (page 42)

5. Eggplant with Sesame Sauce (page 45)

6. Oysters with Ginger Dressing (page 47)

7. Scallops in a Lemon Shell (page 50)

8. Lobster Nuggets (page 53)

9. Stuffed Lotus Root (page 55)

SUSHI

10. Whitebait and Egg Sushi (page 58)

11. Crab Rolls (page 60)

SASHIMI

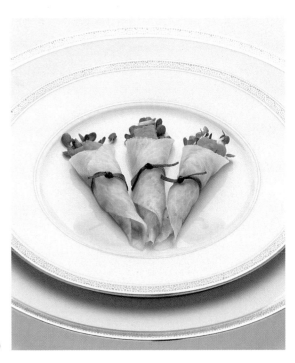

12. Daikon-Wrapped Lox (page 64)

13. Marinated Halibut (page 66)

15. Flounder Sashimi (page 71)

14. Squid Sashimi Rolls (page 69)

16. Halibut Sashimi with Avocado (page 73)

SIMMERED DISHES

17. *Miso*-Braised Abalone (page 76)

18. Dragon's Head (page 78)

19. Broth with Salmon Roe (page 81)

20. Tofu Autumn Mélange (page 83)   21. Turnip with *Miso* (page 85)

22. Oyster Mushrooms in a Kelp Boat (page 87)

STEAMED DISHES

23. Fresh Pea Tofu (page 90)

24. Red Snapper and Buckwheat Noodles (page 93)

25. Sea Urchin Rolls (page 95)

26. Shrimp Noodles (page 97)

27. White Island (page 99)

28. Steamed Red Snapper (page 101)

30. Stuffed Winter Melon (page 106)

29. Tofu Custard with Thick Broth (page 104)

31. Tofu Omelet (page 109)

32. Walnut "Tofu" (page 111)

33. Tofu with *Miso* (page 113)

GRILLED AND
PAN-FRIED DISHES

34. Barbecued Salmon, *Yuan* Style (page 116)

35. Chicken-Stuffed *Matsutake* Mushrooms (page 118)

36. Stones and Moss (page 120)

37. Broiled Sea Urchin (page 122)

38. Glazed Rainbow Trout (page 124)

40. Eggplant with *Miso* (page 128)

39. Stuffed *Shiitake* Mushrooms (page 126)

41. Pan-Fried Scallops (page 130)

42. Pinecone Squid (page 132)

DEEP-FRIED DISHES

43. Deep-Fried *Matsutake* Mushrooms (page 136)

44. Crisp Flounder (page 138)

45. Petrale Sole with Bonito Flakes
(page 140)

46. Scallop *Nori* Rolls (page 142)

47. Prawn Fantasy (page 144)

48. Spring Rain Tempura (page 146)

49. Shrimp in Noodle Basket (page 148)

ASPICS

50. Whitebait in Aspic (page 152)

VINEGARED AND DRESSED DISHES
Sunomono and Aemono

1 Prawns in Golden Cloaks
Ebi no Kimizu-kake

The golden egg yolk sauce (*kimizu*) used in this dish is the Japanese version of hollandaise—without butter. Even in Japanese cooking, one cannot escape the tribulations of attempting to lightly cook eggs into a smooth, creamy sauce. One soon develops an intuition for this kind of sauce, however. The best advice is simply—easy does it.

Oh, yes. The flowers are edible and delicious when dressed with sweet vinegar.

TO SERVE FOUR

GOLDEN SAUCE (*KIMIZU*):
3 egg yolks
2 Tbsps *mirin*
3 Tbsps lemon juice
1 Tbsp sugar
$\frac{1}{8}$ tsp salt

4 prawns with heads
2 tsps salt

GARNISH:
8–12 yellow chrysanthemums (1$\frac{1}{2}$–2 inch diameter)
1 tsp salt
$\frac{1}{3}$ cup flavor vinegar (*sanbai-zu*, page 156)

SPECIAL EQUIPMENT:
double boiler
4 bamboo skewers

Combine the golden-sauce ingredients in top of double boiler. Have a bowl of cold water ready. Cook sauce over low heat while beating with whisk or egg beater until thick. Force cool to room temperature by placing saucepan in bowl of cold water. Cover and refrigerate.

1

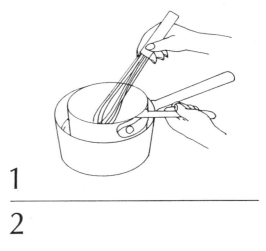

2

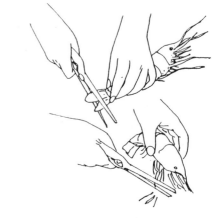

Wash prawns. Cut off tip of tail and tips of legs.

TECHNIQUE: In Step 1, if the mixture starts to get too thick too fast, put the pan in the bowl of cold water immediately and stir vigorously.

Thread a skewer into the underside of each prawn from the tail all the way into the head. This keeps the prawns from curling during cooking.

Remove shell from central section of each prawn, leaving shell intact on head and last section of tail.

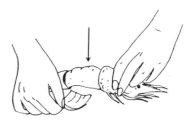

3

5

4

6

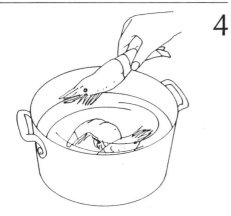

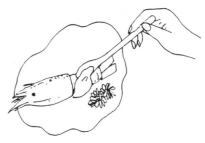

Bring water to boil over high heat in a large saucepan and add salt. Add prawns. Return to boil. Reduce heat to low and simmer uncovered for 4–6 minutes, depending on size of prawns. Do not overcook. Remove skewered prawns and cool. When the prawns are cool enough to handle, pull out skewers with a twisting action.

Prepare chrysanthemums as an edible garnish by blanching flowers in slightly salted (1 tsp salt to 1 quart water) boiling water for 10 seconds, then plunge into cold water. Remove and gently squeeze out water. Just before serving, dress with flavor vinegar. Arrange portions of each ingredient on individual serving plates. Spoon golden sauce over prawns just before serving.

2 Chicken Nest
Tori no Sugomori

This attractive noodle dish uses *harusame*, which is made from potato starch. The filaments become translucent when cooked and fairly glisten on the plate.

Another touch is the use of crumbled hard-boiled egg yolk that has been dry-cooked and sprinkled on top as a garnish. Egg yolk in this form appears frequently in Japanese cooking—sometimes to garnish white-fleshed fish and shellfish sashimi. The flounder sashimi in this book is another example of its use. It can be used attractively on a Western-style spinach salad, for example.

TO SERVE FOUR

$\frac{1}{2}$ **large chicken breast (about 8–10 oz)**
1 hard-boiled egg yolk
20 sprigs trefoil (*mitsuba*) with stems
   (substitute flat-leafed parsley) (optional)

DRESSING:
2 egg yolks
2 tsps *mirin*
1$\frac{1}{2}$ Tbsps rice vinegar
$\frac{1}{4}$ tsp salt

1 Tbsp light soy sauce
1 Tbsp *dashi* #1 (see page 155)
1 Tbsp toasted white sesame seeds
3 oz *harusame* noodles

Place chicken breast in a saucepan and add enough water to cover. Bring to a rapid boil, reduce heat to low, and simmer 5 minutes. Cover and remove from heat. Set aside for 30 minutes.

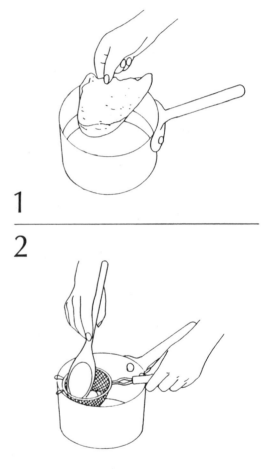

1

2

Force hard-boiled egg yolk through a strainer into a small saucepan. Place over low heat and stir constantly with wooden spoon until dry and granular (about 10–15 minutes). Do not let yolk brown. Set aside.

Cut the leaves from trefoil (or parsley) and discard. Pass stems briefly (10 seconds) through boiling water, then plunge in cold water. Cut into 1½-inch lengths.

Toast sesame seeds lightly in a dry frying pan. Chop thoroughly on dry cutting board. The chopping will release more of their fragrance. Mix into dressing.

3

5

4

6

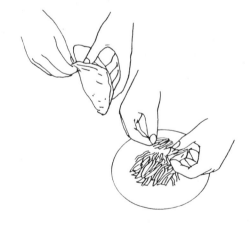

Combine the dressing ingredients in top of double boiler. Place over barely simmering water and stir with a wooden spatula until the mixture starts to resemble mayonnaise. Remove from heat, add soy sauce and *dashi*, mix, and set aside.

Remove skin and bone from cooked chicken breast. Shred with fingers.

Add *harusame* noodles to 1½ quarts cold water in a saucepan. Bring to a rapid boil and cook for about 1 minute. Pour into colander and rinse in cold running water (see TECHNIQUE).

Combine chicken and trefoil in a large bowl. Add dressing and toss.

7

9

8

10

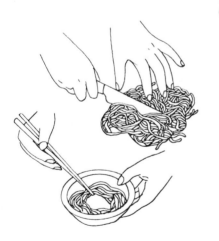

Cut cooked noodles several times, then divide into four portions. Place each portion in individual serving bowl, leaving a space in the center.

Place a portion of chicken mixture in center of each noodle serving. Sprinkle with egg yolk granules and serve.

TECHNIQUE: *Harusame* noodles sometimes stick together after cooking. If this happens, pass them briefly through warm water to loosen. They will disintegrate if allowed to sit in water.

3 Icicle Oysters
Tsurara Sugaki

This delicate oyster dish makes a delightful first course. It uses arrowroot, which lends a marvelously smooth texture to the lightly-cooked oysters. When it is accompanied by the tart sauce, you have a truly different oyster preparation.

TO SERVE FOUR

12 to 20 oysters (about 2 inches)
1 Tbsp flour
¾ cup arrowroot
1 scallion, green part only
3-inch length of daikon radish
¼ tsp cayenne pepper
ice water

SAUCE:

2 Tbsps lemon juice
3 Tbsps *dashi* #1
1 Tbsp rice vinegar
1 Tbsp *mirin*
2 Tbsps soy sauce

Place oysters in bowl, add flour, and mix well. Rinse oysters thoroughly under cold running water. Drain. This important step helps rid oysters of any sand.

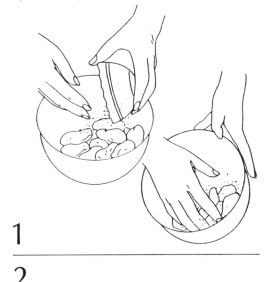

1

2

Place arrowroot on a plate. Carefully coat each oyster and dust off excess starch. Prepare large bowl of ice water.

TECHNIQUE: In Japan, grated daikon is used for cleansing oysters (Step 2). However, flour works just as well and, of course, is more readily available.

Bring 1 quart water to boil in large saucepan.
Reduce heat to medium. Carefully add oysters
and cook until just done (about 2 minutes).

Peel a section of daikon radish and finely grate
enough to garnish each serving with about 2
Tbsps.

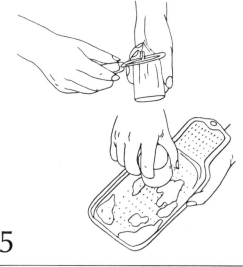

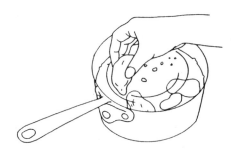

3

5

4

6

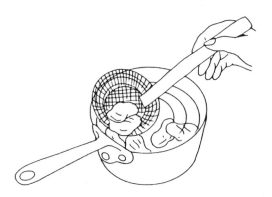

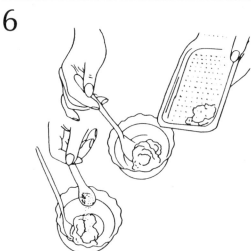

Remove oysters and immediately plunge into
ice water. Drain and set aside.

Place grated radish in small bowl, pour off
excess liquid, and add $\frac{1}{4}$ tsp cayenne pepper
(or more if you like). Mix thoroughly.

Chop green part of scallion into fine rounds (about 2 Tbsps).

Arrange 3–5 oysters in each serving dish in an attractive manner. Carefully spoon about 2 Tbsps sauce around oysters. *Do not* pour sauce over oysters.

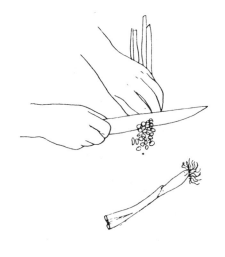

7

9

8

10

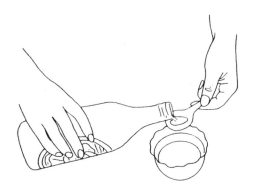

Mix sauce ingredients.

Neatly place grated daikon and chopped scallion on top and serve.

4 Enoki Mushroom Salad with Salmon Caviar
Ikura to Enoki no Aemono

For this salad, fresh enoki mushrooms are used. Enoki are easily cultivated commercially and therefore are rapidly becoming available outside Japan. They are sold in sealed plastic bags, which keep them fresh for about a week or so. This tasty, decorative mushroom has a wide variety of uses.

American sushi bar customers have learned to recognize salmon roe and order it by its Japanese name–*ikura*. Unfortunately, salmon roe comes packaged by mother nature entangled in a membrane that is not easily removed. The hearty salmon fisherman who wants to use the roe fresh from his recent catch is probably best advised to forego it and purchase the processed roe from the market instead.

TO SERVE FOUR

7 oz enoki (snowpuff) mushrooms
$1\frac{1}{2}$ tsps salt
$\frac{1}{2}$ cup salmon roe

DRESSING:
4 kiwi fruit
$\frac{1}{4}$ cup *mirin*
$\frac{1}{4}$ tsp salt

Rinse enoki mushrooms under running water. Bring 1 quart water to a boil and add 1 tsp salt.

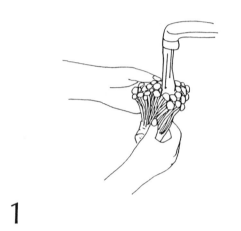

1

2

Have a bowl of cold water nearby. Hold the enoki by the stems as shown. Plunge them into the boiling water then immediately into the cold water. Drain.

Bring 2 cups water to a boil and add $\frac{1}{2}$ tsp salt. Again, have a bowl of cold water nearby. Place salmon roe in a strainer and pour boiling salted water over. Plunge into cold water, drain, and set aside.

Warm *mirin* in a saucepan and ignite with a match. Swish liquid around in pan to burn off all alcohol.

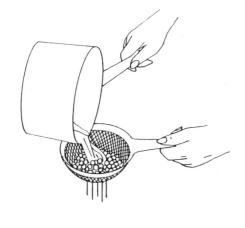

3
5
4
6

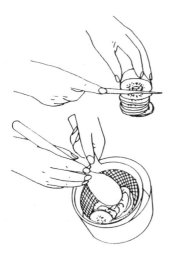

Peel and thinly slice kiwi fruit. Strain through a fine sieve. Discard the seeds.

Add the *mirin* and $\frac{1}{4}$ tsp salt to the strained kiwi fruit and blend.

Trim enoki 1 inch from the bottom.

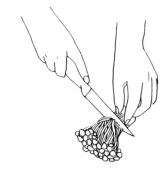

7

8

Toss salmon roe and enoki together. Put portions in the center of individual serving dishes, surround with dressing, and serve.

5 Eggplant with Sesame Sauce
Nasu no Goma-kake

In recent years, a small, 4–5 inch eggplant called the oriental or Japanese eggplant has been showing up in American markets around midsummer. It is similar to the ones grown in Japan in that it is more flavorful and has smaller, more tender seeds than the usual large varieties.

The Japanese know that one of the best ways to enjoy eggplant is to simply broil it over an open flame. Often it will be served with sesame sauce. The nutty, lightly roasted aroma of the sauce blends perfectly with the full-flavored eggplant.

TO SERVE FOUR

SAUCE:

$\frac{1}{2}$ **cup white sesame seeds**

2 Tbsps light soy sauce

6 Tbsps *dashi* #1

$\frac{1}{2}$ **tsp *sansho* powder (optional)**

$\frac{1}{4}$ **tsp sesame oil**

4 Japanese eggplants (4–5 inches long)

SPECIAL EQUIPMENT:

mortar or *suribachi* (Japanese grinding bowl)

Lightly toast the sesame seeds in a dry frying pan until they start to pop (see page 13).

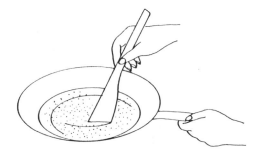

1

2

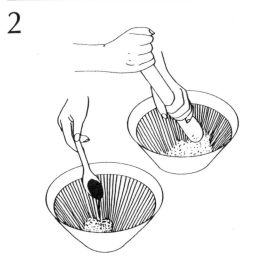

Place toasted seeds in mortar or *suribachi* (Japanese grinding bowl) and grind to an oily paste. Add 1 Tbsp soy sauce at a time and mix well after each addition.

Add *dashi* a little at a time, mixing after each addition. The sauce should be the consistency of heavy cream. Mix in *sansho* powder. Set aside.

Remove from heat. Cut stem end off and remove skin.

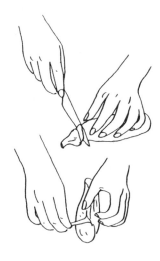

3

5

4

6

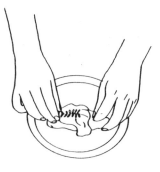

Broil eggplants over an open flame or under the oven broiler until tender and the skin blisters.

Place each eggplant in individual serving dish, spoon sauce over, and serve.

6 Oysters with Ginger Dressing
Kaki no Shoga-zu

This dish uses winter vegetables for a colorful oyster presentation.

TO SERVE FOUR

DRESSING:

2 Tbsps lemon juice
½ tsp ginger juice
2 tsps light soy sauce
1 tsp sugar
1 tsp *mirin*
¼ tsp salt
¼ cup *dashi* #1
½ tsp arrowroot mixed with 1 tsp water

24 oysters (about 1½ to 2 inches)
1 Tbsp flour
1½-inch length of carrot
20 trefoil stems (substitute flat-leafed parsley)
4 oz enoki (snowpuff) mushrooms
4 yellow chrysanthemums (2-inch diameter)
2 Tbsps rice vinegar

Combine dressing ingredients except arrowroot in a small saucepan and bring to a boil. Add arrowroot-water mixture and stir continuously until thickened. Transfer to a bowl and cool to room temperature.

1

2

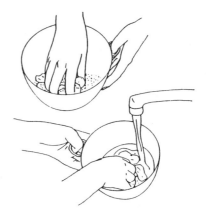

Add flour to the oysters in a bowl and gently mix with the fingers. Rinse with ample changes of water. Drain.

Peel and slice carrot and shred or cut into fine julienne strips.

Cut enoki mushrooms into 1½-inch lengths.

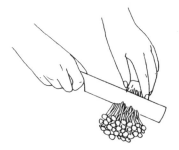

3

5

4

6

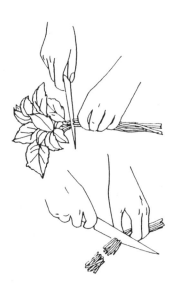

Remove tops from trefoil (or parsley). Cut stems into 1½-inch lengths.

Have a bowl of cold water standing by. Boil water in a saucepan. Add oysters and boil for 1 minute over medium-high heat. Remove oysters with a strainer and immediately plunge into cold water. Change water several times to make sure the oysters are cold. Drain and refrigerate.

Again, have a bowl of cold water standing by. Pluck petals from chrysanthemums. Blanch petals for 10 seconds in boiling water, then plunge into cold water. Drain.

Drain the vegetables well and put in a bowl with 1 Tbsp rice vinegar. Mix well and squeeze out liquid. Do the same with the oysters, but just drain well—do not squeeze.

7

9

8

10

Blanch carrots for 30 seconds and plunge into cold water. Drain. Put trefoil and enoki mushrooms in a strainer and lower them into boiling water. Blanch for 10 seconds then plunge into cold water.

Place 6 oysters on each serving dish and arrange vegetables on top. Spoon dressing over the oysters and vegetables and serve. This dish tastes best when served at room temperature.

TECHNIQUE: Lightly flavoring vegetables or other ingredients with vinegar before they are dressed is an important key to making Japanese style vinegared salads. In Japan this step is called *su arai*–"vinegar wash."

7 Scallops in a Lemon Shell
Kaibashira no Remon-Gama

Because small scallops are so tasty, they are often preferred raw as sushi. As sushi they are prepared in the "battleship" (*gunkan*) style—*nori* seaweed is wrapped to form a cup on top of the rice, into which the tiny scallops are placed. The dark seaweed resembles the iron hull of a warship—very sinister. This cheerier lemon presentation reminds us more of the yellow submarine. Whatever the imagery, the dish demonstrates the attractive possibilities of vinegared foods (*sunomono*).

<u>TO SERVE FOUR</u>

VINEGAR-SOY SAUCE (*NIHAI-ZU*) DRESSING:
2 Tbsps lemon juice
1 Tbsp light soy sauce
1 Tbsp *dashi* #1

4 large lemons
5-inch length of English cucumber
$\frac{1}{2}$ lb fresh bay scallops
1 tsp salt
2 pickling cucumbers
$\frac{3}{4}$ tsp salt
2 tsps *wasabi* powder mixed with $\frac{3}{4}$ tsp water

Combine ingredients for vinegar-soy sauce dressing and set aside. Cut away one-third of the lemons as shown and spoon out the pulp.

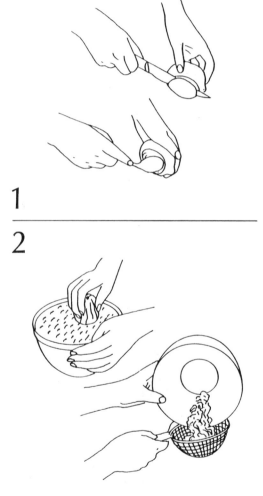

1
_____

2

Grate English cucumber and place in strainer to drain. This should result in about $\frac{1}{2}$ cup of pulp.

To clean the scallops, sprinkle them with 1 tsp salt and mix gently with the fingers. Rinse under cold water and drain.

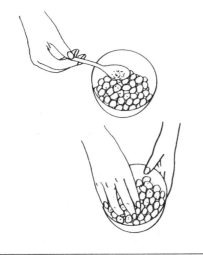

3

Drop pickling cucumbers into boiling water for 30 seconds, then rinse under cold running water until entirely cool. This markes the color more vivid.

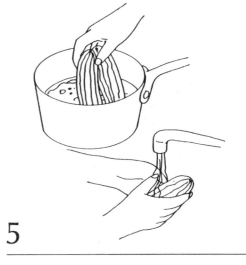

5

4

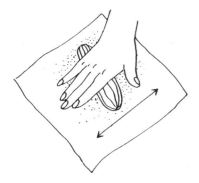

Bring water to a boil in an 8-inch saucepan. Sprinkle $\frac{1}{2}$ tsp salt on a cutting board and roll the pickling cucumbers back and forth several times in salt. Rinse.

6

Slice cucumber very thin. Sprinkle slices with $\frac{1}{4}$ tsp salt, toss until slices are all coated with salt, then leave until they are very limp.

Gently and firmly squeeze out excess liquid.

7

8

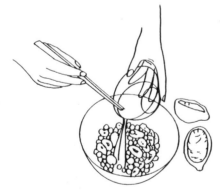

Immediately before serving, toss together
cucumber, scallops, and vinegar-soy sauce.
Spoon into lemon cups and serve with *wasabi*
paste on the side.

TECHNIQUE: In Step 8 it is important that the
dressing not be combined with the other ingredients
until immediately before serving. This insures that
the color of the cucumber stays appetizing. Also, if
left too long, the salt in the soy sauce will draw out
water from the cucumber and make the dressing
watery.

8 Lobster Nuggets
Ise Ebi no Tosa-joyu-zoe

The Japanese hold the lobster in very high regard. The lobster's long feelers resemble a beard. Its rounded back and the tortuous way it swims by bending and straightening are reminiscent of old people. So the lobster has become a symbol of longevity and good luck and often makes its appearance at formal dinners and happy celebrations.

Fresh lobster makes a superb sashimi. For this recipe fresh or frozen lobster tails are used. Buy them undefrosted, so you can control the defrosting process in your refrigerator. It is best to work with the lobster when it is not quite fully thawed.

TO SERVE FOUR

DIPPING SAUCE:

$\frac{1}{2}$ cup Tosa soy sauce (**Tosa-joyu**, see page 157)

2 fresh or high-quality frozen lobster tails (about 1 lb)
arrowroot

STOCK:

2 cups *dashi* #2
$\frac{1}{8}$ tsp salt
1 tsp light soy sauce
2 tsps *mirin*
1 tsp saké

Make the dipping sauce (Tosa soy sauce) and refrigerate until chilled. Cut open the underside of the lobster tails and remove the meat. Try not to damage the top of the shells; they will be used as decorative garnishes. Discard the softer underside of the shells.

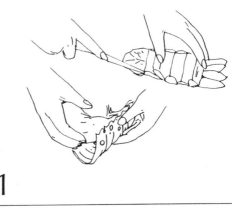

1

2

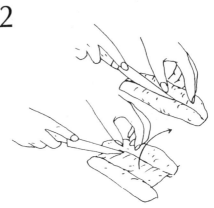

Trim off the red skin of the meat by laying the lobster tail, red side down, flat on the cutting board. Cut the meat down the center lengthwise without cutting through the tail. Then roll, as shown, while trimming off the red part of the meat.

Cut into 1-inch pieces. Combine stock ingredients in saucepan and bring to a boil. Have a bowl of cold water handy.

Cook the shells in the boiling stock until they are bright red. Cut off the tail sections; these will be used as decoration. Other pieces of the shell may be used as well, if you like.

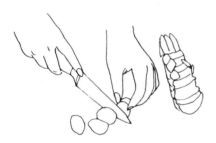

3

5

4

6

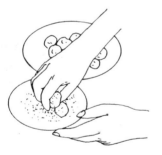

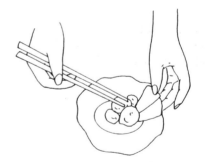

Dust the lobster meat with arrowroot and drop one-fourth of the pieces into boiling stock. Cook until just done (about 1–2 minutes). Remove with a strainer and immediately plunge into cold water. Using only one-fourth of lobster meat each time, repeat for remaining amount.

Place a piece of lobster shell tail on each serving plate and arrange the meat attractively in front of or around it. Place a small amount of dipping sauce in small bowls and serve on the side. Use your choice of garnish. Plate 18 shows blanched mustard flowers dressed with sweet vinegar.

9 Stuffed Lotus Root
Renkon no Kani-zume

The lotus root has been grown in Japan for centuries. The lotus flower is important in Buddhist iconography, and lotus ponds are often found around temples.

The tubular hollows that run through the length of the lotus root make it an unusual and decorative cooking ingredient. In this dish, the hollows are filled with a crab meat mixture. It is dressed with vinegar-soy sauce and garnished with thinly sliced cucumber to make an attractive salad.

TO SERVE FOUR

6-inch length of lotus root (about 2-inch diameter)
2 Tbsps rice vinegar
4 oz cooked crab meat
$\frac{1}{2}$ egg white
1 tsp *mirin*
1 tsp saké
$\frac{1}{8}$ tsp salt

$\frac{1}{4}$ cup vinegar-soy sauce (*nihai-zu*, page 157)

SPECIAL EQUIPMENT:
large mortar or *suribachi* (Japanese grinding bowl)
chopsticks
steamer

Cut the lotus root in half crosswise. Cut and sculpt each piece to form a fluted tubular shape as shown. Add vinegar to 1 quart boiling water, add lotus, and cook 10 minutes.

1

2

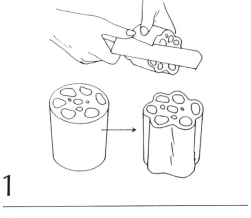

Place the crab and egg white in mortar (or *suribachi*) and work into a thick, stringy mixture with a pestle. Add *mirin*, saké, and salt. Blend well.

TECHNIQUE: A large mortar and pestle or *suribachi* (Japanese grinding bowl) should be used in Step 2. A food processor should be avoided here since there is a danger of creating a paste. The desired result is a stringy mixture that retains some of the crab texture.

Stuff crab mixture into the holes of the lotus
root, tapping down well to eliminate air
pockets. The end of a chopstick is a good tool
for this.

3

4

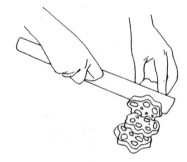

Steam for 15 minutes in a steamer. Cool.
When completely cooled, cut into $\frac{1}{2}$-inch
slices. Arrange slices attractively on individual
serving plates. Spoon vinegar-soy sauce around
base of slices and serve.

SUSHI

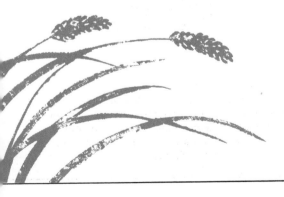

10 Whitebait and Egg Sushi
Shirauo no Kimi-Zushi

*S*hirauo (sold as "whitebait" in American markets) appear in Japan in the spring. They grow from about $2\frac{1}{2}$ to 6 inches long, and, except for the eyes, the body is translucent. When cooked, they turn a milky white, which gives this dish its clean, light look. If whitebait is not available substitute cooked bay shrimp.

The recipe calls for molding the ingredients in a small Japanese wooden press-mold (*oshibako*) with inside dimensions of about $2\frac{1}{2}$ by 5 inches. The top and bottom of the mold are removable, which facilitates demolding. A cake pan (with or without a removable bottom) lined with plastic wrap can substitute. Heavy cardboard, cut to size and also swathed in plastic wrap, will work as a cover upon which a weight can be placed.

TO SERVE FOUR

8 hard-boiled egg yolks
l egg-sized boiling potato
$\frac{1}{4}$ lb raw whitebait (*shirauo*) (substitute cooked bay shrimp)
1 Tbsp salt

SUSHI VINEGAR:

$\frac{1}{4}$ tsp salt
2 tsps sugar
2 Tbsps rice vinegar

SPECIAL EQUIPMENT:

steamer
***oshibako* (wooden mold) or cake pan**
weight (about 2 lbs)

Peel and slice potato and boil until tender. Rinse whitebait and place in bowl with salted water (1 quart water to 1 Tbsp salt). Set aside for 5 minutes.

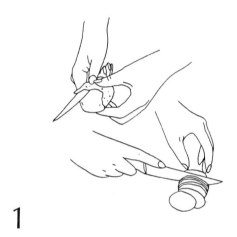

1

2

Drain fish and place in a single layer on a plate small enough to go into a steamer. Steam for 2 minutes. Remove and set aside to cool. Repeat until all fish are cooked. Omit this step if using cooked bay shrimp.

Strain hard-boiled egg yolks through a fine sieve into a bowl. Drain potato and place in cold water to cool. Strain through a fine sieve into the same bowl containing the egg yolk.

Cut heads and tails from fish and lay them on top of the yolk mixture. The fish look best when neatly lined up. Place cover on mold and press for 10 minutes with a weight. Slice and serve.

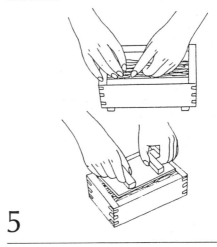

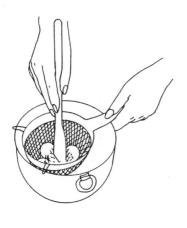

3

5

4

Prepare the sushi vinegar and add to bowl. Mix well with a wooden spoon. Place mixture in a wet *oshibako* (see TECHNIQUE) and use a spatula to make the top flat and even. You may have to do this more than once, depending upon the size of the mold.

TECHNIQUE: The *oshibako* should be soaked in water for about a half-hour before use and then wiped dry. Soaking will prevent food from sticking to the mold. If using a cake or loaf pan, line it with plastic wrap so that the plastic extends over the lip of the pan. Use these loose ends to remove the pressed sushi from the pan.

11 Crab Rolls
Kani no Isobe-maki

Two crabs of identical size may weigh differently. The heavier of the two has more meat and is the one to buy. If scales are not at hand, Japanese chefs will flip the crabs over. They choose the one with the most scratches underneath. Crabs are bottom feeders, and the heavier, more meaty ones ostensibly will be more scratched up.

In this recipe the crab is rolled with a thin layer of egg inside a sheet of *nori* seaweed. Rolling ingredients together in this manner is a time-honored and traditional Japanese method, attractive as well as handy to eat.

TO SERVE FOUR

8 oz cooked crab meat

MARINADE:

2 Tbsps rice vinegar
1 Tbsp *dashi* #1
2 tsps light soy sauce

1 egg
1 sheet *nori* seaweed
1 tsp *wasabi* powder

GARNISH:
sweet-vinegared ginger slices

SPECIAL EQUIPMENT:

Japanese omelet pan (5×7 inches) or 8-inch frying pan
clean kitchen towel or bamboo rolling mat (*makisu*)

Shred crab meat with fingers.

1

2

Combine marinade ingredients and pour over crab meat.

Beat egg with 1 Tbsp water and pour half of this into greased Japanese omelet pan. Cook over medium-low heat until the surface of egg is dry.

Toast *nori* sheet with a slow fanning motion above medium heat. It is done when it becomes crisp and begins to look greenish instead of black against the light.

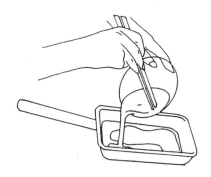

3

5

4

6

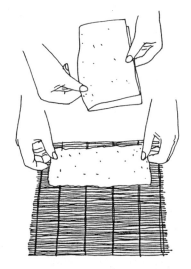

Remove from pan and repeat again with the remaining egg. You will have two relatively thin egg sheets.

Cut *nori* in half crosswise and lay one half on dry kitchen towel folded in half or fourths (or use a bamboo rolling mat—*makisu*)

TECHNIQUE: In Step 3, a Japanese omelet pan is used to produce neat, rectangular egg sheets. An 8-inch frying pan may be substituted and the egg sheet cut and pieced together on the *nori* (Step 7). Since the egg is rolled inside the *nori* and crab, the patchwork will not show.

Trim one egg sheet so that it will cover all but $\frac{1}{2}$ inch of the *nori*, as shown. Lay egg on *nori*.

Roll it like a jellyroll. Leave roll in towel (or mat) for 5 minutes to firm. Repeat with remaining ingredients.

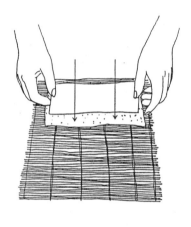

7

9

8

10

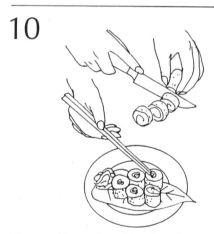

Squeeze marinade from crab meat and spread one-half of meat evenly over egg sheet.

Mix *wasabi* powder with a few drops of water to form a stiff paste. Cut rolls into bite-sized pieces, and serve slices on individual plates with a small dab of *wasabi* paste on top of each slice. Serve small dishes of soy sauce on the side. Sweet-vinegared ginger slices may be used as garnish.

SASHIMI

12 Daikon-Wrapped Lox
Sake no Hosho-maki

In Japanese food parlance, *hosho-maki* refers to wrapping food in something white. Here the salmon and sprouts are wrapped in a thin, white slice of daikon. This dish is finger food and good either as an hors d'oeuvre or as a first course.

An effort should be made to find daikon sprouts for this recipe. They are also known as "spice sprouts" and will add just the right zesty, spicy touch. Cucumber cut into julienne strips may be used in place of daikon sprouts for a milder flavor.

TO SERVE FOUR

12 5 × $\frac{1}{8}$-inch *konbu* kelp strips
3-inch length of daikon radish
$\frac{1}{2}$ tsp salt
4 oz lox, cut in $\frac{1}{3}$-inch widths
daikon sprouts (or julienned English cucumber)

SAUCE:
2 Tbsps rice vinegar
2 Tbsps sugar
1 Tbsp *dashi* #1
pinch salt

Soak *konbu* strips in water. Peel daikon and shape it into an even cylinder.

1

2

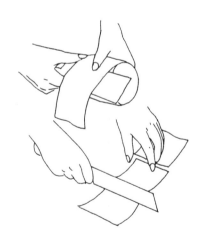

With a *very* sharp knife, peel the daikon into a long thin strip the width of the cylinder. The strip should be almost transparent (see TECHNIQUE). Cut the strip into 12 3 × 3-inch squares.

TECHNIQUE: Cutting (peeling, really) this thin strip of daikon is a difficult technique to master. It helps to use a *very* sharp Japanese chef's vegetable knife. An alternative is to buy a large daikon (5–6 inches in diameter) and make very thin round slices from one end.

Sprinkle daikon slices with $\frac{1}{2}$ tsp salt and set aside until they become pliable. Rinse off salt and pat dry.

Fold the daikon over as shown. The daikon should be folded left side over right—the same way a man buttons his shirt.

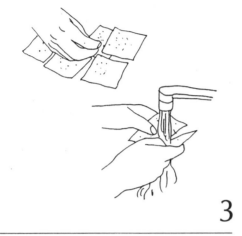

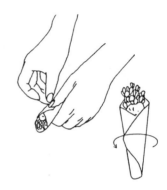

3

5

4

6

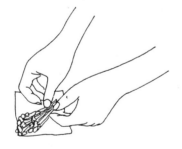

Lay a few sprouts in middle of each sheet of daikon. Place $\frac{1}{12}$ of the lox in the center.

Tie with a piece of *konbu* and arrange attractively on each plate. Mix sauce ingredients until sugar and salt dissolve. Spoon over and serve.

13 Marinated Halibut
Hirame no Kobujime

R aw fish is probably the first thing many Americans associate with Japanese food. Sashimi is certainly a startling idea if you have not tried it. But it is becoming so familiar in the United States that we have included a few variations to the usual presentation here.

This time the sashimi is marinated (packed might be a better word) in seaweed that has been coated with rice vinegar. The result is then served with plum vinegar (*uma-zu*) sauce. *Uma-zu* means "delicious vinegar" in Japanese. You will not be disappointed.

TO SERVE FOUR

2 (or more) sheets dried *konbu* kelp (to fit into cake pan)
rice vinegar
cheesecloth
1 lb freshest halibut fillet
plum vinegar (see page 156)
2 tsps *wasabi* powder mixed with ¾ tsp water to form a stiff paste

SPECIAL EQUIPMENT:

cake pan
weight (about 3 lbs)

Brush *konbu* kelp to remove any sand. Cut each sheet to fit into cake pan.

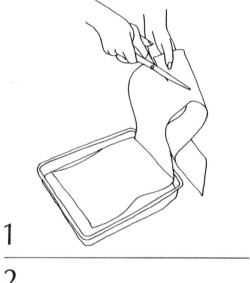

1

2

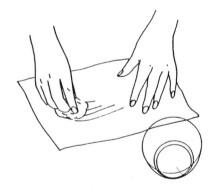

Dip a clean piece of cheesecloth into rice vinegar. Squeeze out excess vinegar and wipe both sides of the *konbu*.

TECHNIQUE: Never wash or rinse *konbu*, because you will loose much of the delicate flavor. Brushing or wiping with a damp cloth is all that is needed.

Cut halibut fillet in half, then into $\frac{1}{4}$-inch-thick slanted slices, as shown.

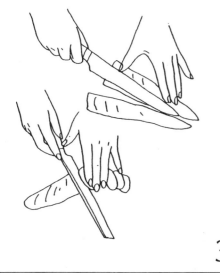

3

Cover the assembly with a sheet of stiff plastic, or another flat-bottomed pan. Place a 3-pound weight on top and refrigerate for 3–5 hours. Prepare plum vinegar.

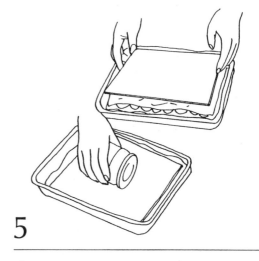

5

4

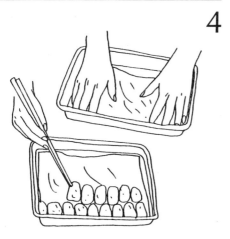

Cover the bottom of pan with *konbu*. Cover the *konbu* with a layer of halibut slices, then cover halibut with second sheet of *konbu*. Several layers of halibut and *konbu* may be necessary, depending on size of pan.

6

When ready to serve, remove from refrigerator and gently peel the fish slices from the *konbu*. For easier handling, dip fingers in rice vinegar.

Arrange attractively on individual dishes.

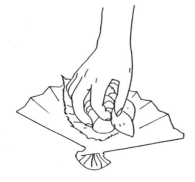

7

8

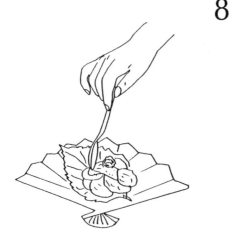

Spoon on plum vinegar sauce, top with *wasabi* paste, and serve. A little *wasabi* paste is eaten with each slice in same manner as horseradish with roast beef.

14 Squid Sashimi Rolls
Ika no Naruto-zukuri

A squid dish has been chosen for the final sashimi variation because there is nothing quite like biting into raw squid, unless it is biting into raw squid wrapped around vinegared chrysanthemums.

Truly fresh squid has a slightly translucent appearance. Also, the thin skin is covered with tiny blackish-brown spots. As the squid ages, these spots begin to disappear, and the skin becomes more whitish and opaque.

You will have leftover cuttings (tip and legs) from this recipe. These are wonderful when broiled (see Pinecone Squid, page 132).

TO SERVE FOUR

**5 large yellow chrysanthemums (about 1$\frac{1}{2}$
cups)**
1 tsp salt
2 squid (body length about 6 inches)
1 sheet *nori* seaweed

GARNISH:
2 tsps finely grated fresh ginger root

Wash chrysanthemums and remove petals. Discard centers. Bring 1 quart water to a boil and add 1 tsp salt. Add chrysanthemum petals and blanch, while stirring, for 10 seconds. Drain into a colander and rinse in cold water. If there is a residual bitter taste, rinse longer. Drain and squeeze off water. Set aside.

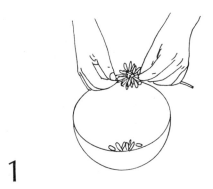

1

2

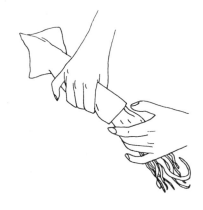

Gently pull the tentacles out of each squid. Wash. Save the tentacles for other dishes.

Slice each body open so that it lays flat. Clean away innards, then trim flesh into rectangles about the size of a half-sheet of *nori* cut crosswise.

Place each squid rectangle on a half-sheet of *nori*, scored side up. Turn over so that the *nori* side is up and lay one-half of the blanched chrysanthemum petals along the near edge.

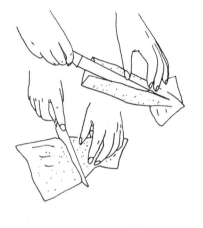

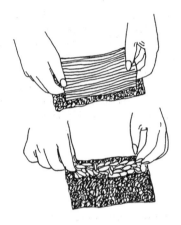

3

5

4

6

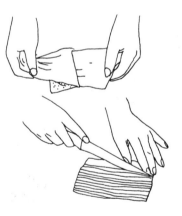

Pull off skin with fingers. Score skin side to two-thirds the depth of the squid flesh at about $\frac{1}{4}$-inch intervals. Wash thoroughly and pat dry. Cut *nori* sheet in half crosswise.

Roll up tightly and cut into $\frac{1}{2}$-inch slices. Serve with grated ginger and small dishes of soy sauce on the side. The ginger is to be mixed with soy sauce at the table and used as a dip.

15 Flounder Sashimi
Karei no Kogane-ae

Normally, sashimi is served with no culinary manipulations. The essence of sashimi is to enjoy it on its own terms—absolutely fresh, flavorful, and unembellished, save for a light touch of soy sauce and *wasabi*.

Occasionally, however, it is nice to stray from the path. In this case, two departures are made. First, the flounder is coated with dry-cooked egg yolk, which provides a bright, decorative yellow. Second, the conventional dipping sauce is changed to a mixture of pickled plum (*umeboshi*) and soy sauce—a tart, unusual variation.

TO SERVE FOUR

3 hard-boiled egg yolks
8 oz freshest flounder (or other flatfish) fillet

DIPPING SAUCE:
10 pickled plums (*umeboshi*)
soy sauce

Strain egg yolks through a sieve into a saucepan.

1

2

Stirring constantly, cook yolk over low heat until completely dry. Spread on a plate to cool and set aside. (The yolk should resemble poppy seeds.)

Slice fish into bite-sized pieces. Refrigerate
until ready to serve.

Just before serving, roll the fish in egg yolk.
Serve on lettuce or a leaf from the garden for
a striking yellow-green contrast. Provide
dipping sauce in small bowls on the side.

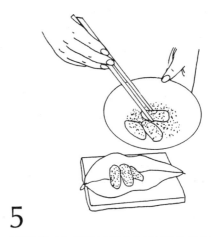

3 | **5**

4

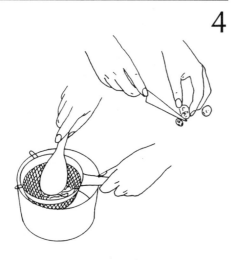

Remove seeds from pickled plums and strain
flesh through a fine sieve. Blend in soy sauce a
little at a time, until the mixture resembles
thick cream.

16 Halibut Sashimi with Avocado
Hirame to Avocado

It is exciting to watch how talented, young Western chefs are adapting traditional recipes from Japan. This sashimi variation is a California creation, though avocado has already made its debut in some Tokyo sushi parlors. In any case, the avocado's smooth creamy texture is a wonderful accompaniment to the fish.

A little ginger root and bits of red chili are being used in place of *wasabi*, a decorative deviation from the traditional. The visual quality of the avocado is important. To insure that you do not have bruised fruit, it is best to buy hard avocados and let them soften in your own kitchen.

TO SERVE FOUR

$\frac{1}{2}$-inch piece fresh ginger root
1 small dried red chili, seeded
$\frac{1}{2}$ lb freshest halibut fillet
1 ripe avocado
lemon juice

DIPPING SAUCE:
Tosa soy sauce (*Tosa-joyu*, see page 157)

Prepare Tosa soy sauce. Peel and finely grate ginger. Set both aside.

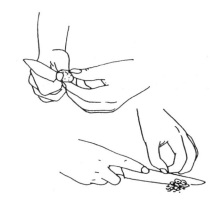

1

2

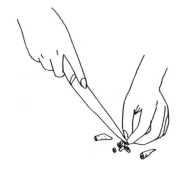

Cut seeded chili into fine rounds. Set aside. (Be sure to wash your hands thoroughly after handling chilies. The oil can easily irritate the skin or get into your eyes.)

Cut halibut in half lengthwise.

Cut avocado in half; remove seed and peel. Cut into $\frac{1}{2}$-inch angled slices as shown. It is best to serve this dish right away, but if it is being prepared ahead, the avocado should be brushed with a little lemon juice to prevent it from browning.

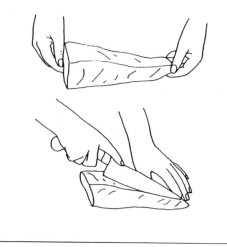

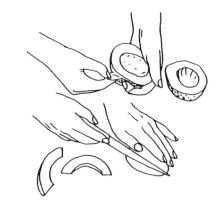

3

5

4

6

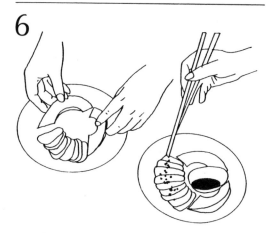

Cut fish into $\frac{1}{2}$-inch slices. Your knife should be very sharp, and each slice should be a clean, single cut. Handle the fish as little as possible.

Arrange attractively on individual plates as shown. Place dipping sauce in a small container. Sprinkle ginger and chili over fish. If you prefer, omit these two and serve *wasabi* paste on the side, which is to be mixed into the dipping sauce.

SIMMERED DISHES
Nimono

17 *Miso*-Braised Abalone
Awabi no Miso-ni

With the price of abalone being what it is, this recipe is probably an exercise in wishful thinking unless you are very rich or a very good abalone diver. But since abalone is prized in Japanese cuisine, at least one recipe using the live mollusk is surely called for.

In addition to *awabi*, its common name in Japanese, abalone is also referred to as *namagai*—"raw shellfish"—which means a shellfish best served as sashimi or in a vinegared "salad."

TO SERVE FOUR

1 medium abalone
salt
saké
8-inch length of daikon radish
1 Tbsp *miso*
1 Tbsp soy sauce

Rinse the abalone. Loosen the meat by inserting a strong thin metal blade between the shell and the flesh at the pointed end.

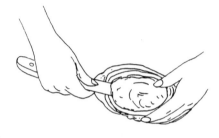

1

2

Hold the pointed end up with the left hand and the meat with the right. Slam the shell down against the work surface a couple of times to free the meat.

Remove and discard the innards. Sprinkle flesh with salt and rub it in, then scrub well under running water with a brush.

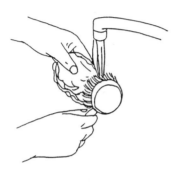

3

Remove and discard daikon and continue cooking, covered, for 3 more hours, turning occasionally. Add enough saké to double the volume of pot liquid. Cook for another hour. Add *miso* and soy sauce and cook, uncovered, until almost all of the liquid is reduced. Check frequently to prevent burning. Spoon sauce over abalone occasionally.

5

4

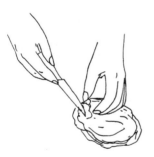

Cut the mouth off (opposite side from innards). The abalone is now ready to be cooked or sliced into sashimi. Peel and cut the daikon into 1-inch-thick rounds. Place abalone and daikon in a saucepan with enough water to cover by 1 inch. Bring to a boil and reduce heat to low. Cover and cook for 1 hour.

6

Cool in saucepan. Wipe *miso* off abalone and trim rough edges all around. Slice into $\frac{1}{4}$-inch slices. Stand several slices on edge on individual serving dishes (see Plate 17). Serve with a garnish of blanched mustard flowers or sliced cucumbers.

TECHNIQUE: The daikon in this recipe performs two functions: it acts as a flavoring agent and also as a tenderizer for the abalone. Without it, the abalone would be unpleasantly tough.

18 Dragon's Head
Hiryozu no Kuzu-an

One definition of creativity is to look at something and see something else. Someone in Japan looked at this little delicacy and, rather than seeing a knobby tofu lump, saw a dragon's head. The name has stuck.

Whatever the visual associations, this dish is another superlative example of the many uses of tofu. In this case, it acts as a binder for a number of tasty surprises—*shiitake* mushroom, ginkgo nuts (or peas), and carrot. The dumpling is deep-fried and served in a thick sauce.

TO SERVE FOUR

2 × 4 × 3-inch cake regular tofu
4 small fresh (or dried and reconstituted) *shiitake* mushrooms
1½-inch length of carrot
20 fresh ginkgo nuts (substitute ¼ cup fresh peas)
1 egg white
½ tsp salt
2 tsps sugar
vegetable oil for deep-frying

SAUCE:

1 cup *dashi* #1
2 Tbsps light soy sauce
2 Tbsps *mirin*
1 Tbsp saké

1 tsp hot mustard powder
2 tsps arrowroot

SPECIAL EQUIPMENT:

cheesecloth or clean kitchen towel
weight (1–2 dinner plates)
bowl or *suribachi* (Japanese grinding bowl)

Wrap tofu in cheesecloth or a clean kitchen towel and place on a slanted cutting board. Weight (with a dinner plate or two) and allow to drain for about 30 minutes.

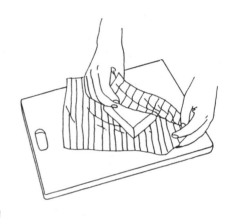

1

2

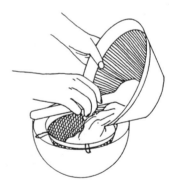

Mince *shiitake* mushrooms and cut carrot into julienne strips. Shell ginkgo nuts (see TECHNIQUE). Chop nuts coarsely. Mash tofu in a bowl (or *suribachi*). Add egg white and blend into mashed tofu. Force tofu through a fine sieve, then add salt, sugar, carrot, and ginkgo nuts. Mix well.

TECHNIQUE: After shelling ginkgo nuts, the inner skin can be loosened for easy removal by dropping them in a saucepan of boiling water. Remove pan from heat, leaving ginkgo nuts immersed until cool.

Heat oil to 350°F. Divide tofu mixture into fourths. Scoop up each fourth with a large spoon and form a flattish dumpling.

Boil 1 quart water. Place deep-fried tofu dumplings in a colander and pour the boiling water over them. This removes excess oil.

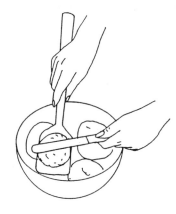

3

5

4

6

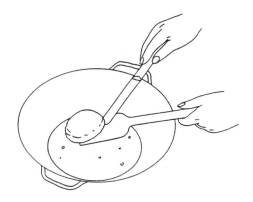

Gently drop dumpling into hot oil and fry until deep golden brown (dumpling will puff). Remove and drain. Fry remaining three portions of tofu in the same manner.

Combine the sauce ingredients in a large saucepan. Bring to a boil over high heat, add dumplings, cover, and simmer over low heat for 30 minutes.

Mix mustard powder with a bit of water to make a soft paste. Cover and set aside.

Increase heat to medium. Add 1 Tbsp cold water to arrowroot and mix well. Mix a little warm sauce into arrowroot and pour mixture into sauce, stirring constantly until thickened. This process prevents the sauce from becoming lumpy.

7

9

8

10

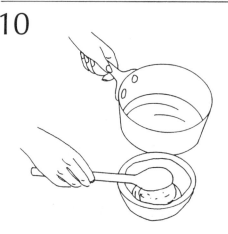

Gently remove dumplings and place in individual serving bowls. Keep warm.

Spoon one-fourth of the sauce over each dumpling and serve with a dab of hot mustard on top. The mustard should be spread over the dumpling before eating for that bright spicy touch. Non-mustard lovers can forego this step and remove the dab.

19 Broth with Salmon Roe
Ikura no Suimono

The Japanese look to Hokkaido, the northernmost (and coldest) island for their finest salmon catch. So it is not surprising that this dish originates there.

It should be made in winter when the salmon are tastiest and the roe abundant. Daikon is also tastiest at this time of the year, so this is truly a winter dish.

TO SERVE FOUR

$\frac{1}{2}$ lb fresh salmon
$\frac{1}{4}$ tsp salt
4-inch length of daikon radish
$\frac{1}{8}$ tsp fresh ginger juice
1 tsp light soy sauce
2 tsps saké
1$\frac{1}{2}$ tsps arrowroot
6 Tbsps salmon caviar
salt
2 Tbsps minced scallions, green part only

Slice the salmon into bite-sized pieces (about 28 pieces). Sprinkle with salt and set aside for 1 hour.

1

2

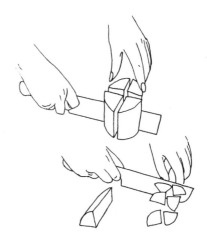

Peel daikon and quarter it lengthwise. Cut crosswise into $\frac{1}{4}$-inch-thick slices.

Place daikon in 3 cups water, bring to a boil over high heat, then reduce heat to low and simmer, uncovered, until just tender. Drain (discard pot liquor) and rinse in cold water. This process rids daikon of its strong odor. Return daikon to saucepan, add 2 cups water, ginger juice, soy sauce, and saké and cook over low heat until daikon is hot.

Mix arrowroot with 1 Tbsp water and slowly add to broth, stirring constantly and gently. Be careful not to break up the salmon. When the soup thickens, add the caviar. At this point adjust seasoning to taste. Let liquid come to a boil and remove from heat immediately.

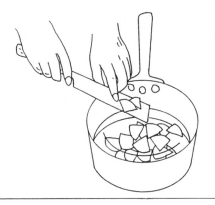

3

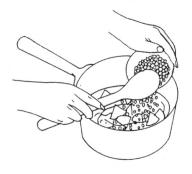

5

4

6

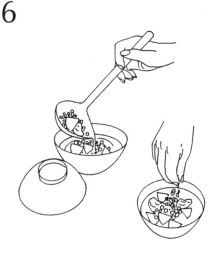

Add the salmon to the daikon and cook for 5 minutes over low heat or until the salmon is just cooked.

Ladle soup into serving bowls and sprinkle with minced scallion. Serve immediately.

20 Tofu Autumn Mélange
Tofu no Matsutake Ankake

The *matsutake* mushroom is highly prized in Japan and is associated with the coming of autumn. So far, no one has discovered a way to cultivate these mushrooms, so they must be gathered wild, in pine forests. In California, Washington, and Oregon they are gathered commercially by professional mushroom hunters. Most are exported to Japan. In the U.S. they are available primarily at Japanese and Korean food stores and some gourmet shops.

Matsutake is enjoyed for its subtle fragrance, which centers in the cap, and for its flavor, which concentrates in the stem. Tofu is a good choice to complement it, since tofu's simple flavor does not interfere with the mushroom's delicacy.

This dish, with its assortment of carrot, beans, bits of chicken, and *matsutake* on a base of white tofu, makes a colorful, light first course.

TO SERVE FOUR

4 × 5 × 2-inch cake regular tofu
1 cup *konbu dashi* (see page 156)
2 oz chicken breast meat
4-inch carrot
20 snow peas
carrot garnishes (optional; see page 88)
2 *matsutake* mushrooms (2 oz each)
2 cups *dashi* #1
2 tsps *mirin*
1 Tbsp sugar
1 tsp salt
2 tsps soy sauce
1 Tbsp arrowroot mixed with 2 Tbsps water

Cut tofu into four pieces. Cook tofu, covered, in *konbu dashi* for 5 minutes over low heat. Set aside in covered saucepan.

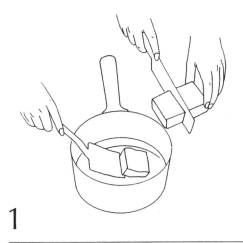

1

2

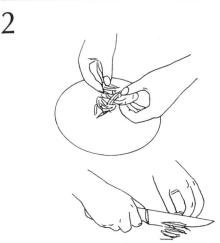

Shred the chicken, julienne carrots and snow peas. Make carrot garnishes (see page 88) if desired.

Trim off bottoms of mushroom stems and rinse mushrooms under cold running water. Do not rub the cap too much.

Combine *dashi* #1, *mirin*, sugar, salt and soy sauce in a saucepan over medium heat. Add chicken, julienned carrot, and carrot garnishes. Cook for 2 minutes or until solid ingredients are just done. Add snow peas, mushroom, and arrowroot-water mixture. Cook, stirring constantly, until sauce thickens.

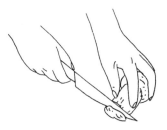

3

5

4

6

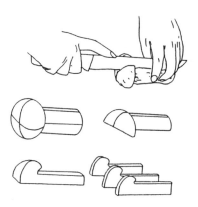

Slice *matsutake* as shown.

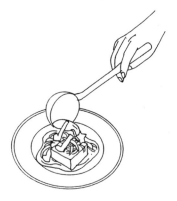

Place one piece of tofu on each plate. Spoon one-fourth of *matsutake* mixture with pot liquor, over tofu and serve.

21 Turnip with *Miso*
Kabu no Dengaku

In some parts of the world, turnips are one of the few vegetables available in winter. The French serve them braised, pureed, glazed, and even in casseroles. To this list, the Japanese add *Kabu no Dengaku*. The turnip is cooked in *dashi* and combined with the flavors of grated lemon rind and *miso*.

Smaller turnips are more suitable for this dish. If you can find turnips with their greens, leave about an inch of stem attached when you cut them off. This adds color and freshness to the presentation.

TO SERVE FOUR

4 turnips
6–8 cups *dashi* #2
1 lemon

SAUCE:
½ cup white *miso*
1 Tbsp sugar
3 Tbsps *mirin*
2 Tbsps *dashi* #1
1 egg yolk
2 Tbsps finely chopped walnuts

Cut the greens from turnips, leaving about 1 inch of stem remaining. Wash thoroughly, being especially careful to clean all dirt from stem bases. Cut turnip about one-fourth of the way down from the top as shown. Cut each turnip body, including severed top one-fourth, into six facets. If turnip wobbles, slice the base to flatten.

1

2

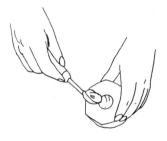

Scoop about 1 Tbsp of flesh from the center of each turnip.

Place in a saucepan with enough *dashi* to cover. Cover with a drop-lid and cook over medium heat for 10 minutes. At this point, remove severed tops to avoid overcooking them and reserve. Continue cooking turnips until just tender; do not allow them to get mushy.

Combine the sauce ingredients in a saucepan. Cook over low heat while stirring with a wooden spoon until thick and shiny (about 10 minutes). Remove from heat and add grated lemon zest.

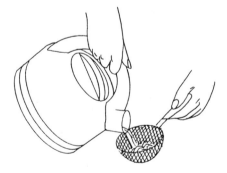

3 5

4 6

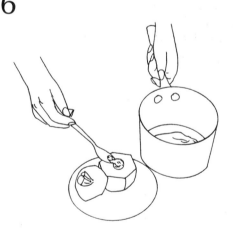

Grate lemon zest from one whole lemon. Place zest in a fine strainer and pour boiling water over it. Drain and set aside.

Spoon sauce into the cavity of each turnip. Place on individual serving dishes. Lean the turnip tops against the bodies as shown in Plate 21. Serve warm.

22 Oyster Mushrooms in a Kelp Boat
Shimeji no Nibitashi

O yster mushrooms (*shimeji*) are a
wonderful mushroom variety that can be
easily cultivated and made available
throughout the year. They are known for their
flavor, compared to a mushroom such as the
matsutake (page 83), which is prized for its
fragrance.

In restaurants in Japan, this dish is often
served on a small individual charcoal brazier
(*shichirin*). The *konbu* kelp boat containing the
stock is placed on top of the brazier. Each
guest then cooks his own tasty mushrooms.
This recipe calls for the oyster mushrooms to
be cooked in stock in the kitchen and then
served in the *konbu* boat. These small
individual braziers are turning up in oriental
stores. If you can find them, they are
wonderful for individual table cooking such as
barbecuing meat, shrimp, oysters, etc.

TO SERVE FOUR

1 lb oyster mushrooms (*shimeji*)
8 5-inch lengths of gourd ribbon (*kampyo*)
4 5×10-inch sheets of *konbu* kelp
1½ cups *dashi* #1
¾ tsp salt
2 tsps light soy sauce
2 tsps saké
lemon zest
carrot garnish (optional)

SPECIAL EQUIPMENT:

garnish cutters (see TECHNIQUE)

Rinse mushrooms; cut off and discard tough
bottom. Set aside.

1

2

Soak gourd ribbon in warm water for 5
minutes. Wipe *konbu* with a damp cloth. Do
not wash.

When each sheet of *konbu* becomes pliable, gather the ends and tie it into a boat shape with 2 gourd ribbons (see Plate 22).

Add mushrooms and bring the pot liquor back to a boil, then remove from heat. Serve hot with a bit of pot liquor in individual *konbu* boats. Garnish with a twist of lemon zest.

3

5

4

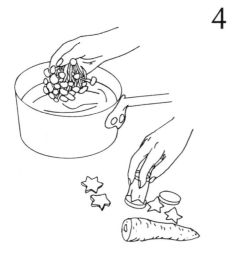

Combine *dashi*, salt, soy sauce, and saké in a large saucepan. Bring to a boil over medium heat. Make the carrot garnishes (see TECHNIQUE) and add.

TECHNIQUE: Carrot garnishes are optional and recommended purely for visual appeal. They can be made with inexpensive metal garnish cutters, something like small cookie cutters, that come in assorted decorative shapes. They are sold in most cooking stores. You may also cut slices from a length of carrot sculpted to form the desired cross-sections (flower, leaf, etc.). If added, however, they need longer cooking than the mushrooms, which cook quickly. Do not add the mushrooms in Step 5 until carrot is tender.

STEAMED DISHES
Mushimono

23 Fresh Pea Tofu
Aomame Dofu

Tofu's superlative quality is its very plainness. It sets off the flavor of accompanying foods in the way that an artist's neutral grays enliven his color accents. This delicate summer first course takes advantage of that quality by blending a puree of summer's fresh peas into the tofu.

TO SERVE FOUR

10-inch bar agar-agar (*kanten*)
4 × 2½ × 1¾-inch cake silk tofu
1 tsp salt
1 cup shelled fresh peas
1 cup *dashi* #2

SAUCE:

¾ cup *dashi* #1
¼ cup light soy sauce
1 Tbsp saké
1 Tbsp *mirin*

GARNISH:

lemon peel slivers
***wasabi* powder (optional)**

SPECIAL EQUIPMENT:

cheesecloth or clean kitchen towel
weight (about 2 lbs)
food processor or blender
5 × 6 × 2-inch pan (see TECHNIQUE)

Tear agar-agar into small pieces and soak in water to cover for at least 2 hours.

1

2

In order to drain water from the tofu, place it on a slanted cutting board. Wrap in cheesecloth or clean kitchen towel and place two dinner plates or a weight (about 2 pounds) on top. Leave for 15 minutes.

TECHNIQUE: A shallow metal pan is used as a mold in this recipe. To facilitate demolding, the pan should be wet before mixture is poured in. Nonstick sprays should not be used. The pan may also be set briefly in warm water. Molds of any decorative shape (jello molds, cups, ice cube trays, etc.) may be used.

Bring 1 quart water to boil. Add 1 tsp salt and peas and cook over high heat for 4–5 minutes, depending on size of peas. They should be just tender, not mushy.

Place *dashi* #2 in saucepan. Squeeze water out of agar-agar and add it (agar-agar) to *dashi*. Cook over low heat until the agar-agar dissolves, then remove from heat.

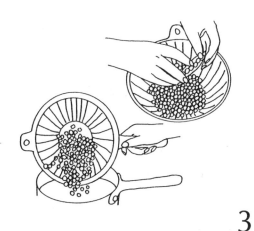

3

5

4

6

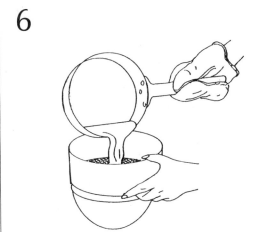

Empty peas into a colander and immediately rinse under cold running water to halt further cooking. Peel each pea by pressing it gently between the thumb and index finger. The soft inside will pop out. Place peeled peas in food processor or blender and puree. Set aside. Similarly, puree tofu until creamy. Set aside.

Pour mixture through a sieve into a bowl.

Add pureed peas and mix thoroughly. Set aside until mixture cools to room temperature.

Wet shallow pan with water and pour in tofu mixture. It should be about $\frac{1}{2}$ to $\frac{3}{4}$ inch deep. Cool to room temperature then cover with plastic wrap. Refrigerate until chilled.

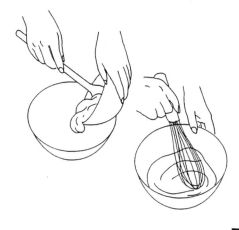

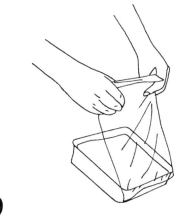

7

9

8

10

Blend in the tofu until a uniform color is achieved.

Combine sauce ingredients in a saucepan and bring to a boil. Chill. Demold the chilled tofu mixture and cut into any desired shape. Place on individual serving plates and spoon sauce around base. Garnish with lemon peel slivers. Serve chilled. This dish may also be served with a little *wasabi* paste to be eaten together with tofu and sauce.

24 Red Snapper and Buckwheat Noodles
Tai no Soba-mushi

In Japan, buckwheat noodles are popular fare and are served either hot in a broth or cold with a dipping sauce.

In this dish, buckwheat noodles attractively wrapped around fish provide a light first course.

TO SERVE FOUR

10 oz red snapper filiet
$\frac{1}{8}$ tsp salt
1 tsp saké
1 scallion, green part only
4 oz dried buckwheat noodles (*soba*)
20 snow peas

SAUCE:

1$\frac{1}{2}$ cups *konbu dashi* (see page 156)
$\frac{1}{4}$ cup *mirin*
3 Tbsps light soy sauce

SPECIAL EQUIPMENT:

steamer
string

Cut fish into 4 pieces. Sprinkle both sides with salt and saké and set aside for 10 minutes.

1

2

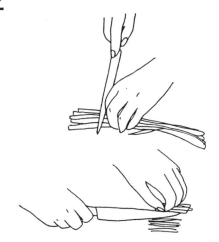

Cut scallion into 2-inch lengths and julienne into needle-thin strips. Place in a bowl of cold water and set aside.

Have another large bowl of cold water ready. Bring 2 quarts water to a boil in a saucepan. Tie one-fourth of buckwheat noodles at one end as shown. Boil two bunches at a time for 3 minutes. Remove with a strainer and plunge into cold water to prevent further cooking. Drain.

Wrap fish pieces with noodles, as shown. Place on plate with overlapping noodle side down and steam in a preheated steamer at medium-high heat for 3–4 minutes, depending upon thickness of fish.

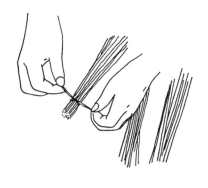

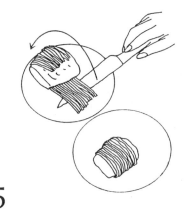

3

5

4

6

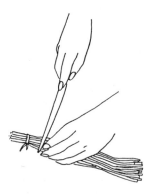

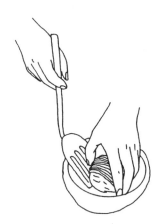

Combine *konbu dashi*, *mirin*, and soy sauce in a saucepan and bring to a boil. Turn heat to low and keep warm. Cut off tied end of noodles and discard.

Remove noodle-wrapped fish to serving bowls. Strain liquid from the steamed fish into the sauce. Correct seasoning to taste. Pour sauce around each piece of noodle-wrapped fish. Drain scallion and garnish each serving. Serve hot.

TECHNIQUE: Tying the buckwheat noodles before boiling is a simple, effective way to keep them untangled during the cooking process so that the wrapping procedure can be accomplished easily. It is a method that can be used for any kind of noodle presentation.

25 Sea Urchin Rolls
Uni no Neritama-maki

S ea urchin remains an exotic delicacy for
most Americans. This presentation of it is
very unusual even by Japanese standards.

The egg and sea urchin combination is quite
a rich marriage—much richer than is normally
found in Japanese cuisine. It should be served
without sauce, since the egg yolk is seasoned
and the sea urchin is naturally moist. Three
slices make a generous serving.

TO SERVE FOUR

1 whole egg
3 egg yolks
$\frac{1}{4}$ cup *mirin*
3 Tbsps rice vinegar
$\frac{1}{4}$ tsp salt
**2 containers fresh sea urchin (sold in small
    wooden trays)**

SPECIAL EQUIPMENT:
double boiler
**bamboo rolling mat (*makisu*) or clean kitchen
    towel (folded in half or quarters)**
plastic wrap
steamer

Beat egg and egg yolks well. Strain through
fine sieve into top of double boiler. Add
beaten egg and yolks, *mirin*, vinegar, and salt
and blend.

1

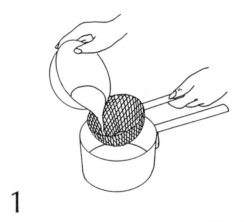

2

Cook over barely simmering hot water, stirring
with a wooden spatula until the mixture comes
cleanly off the sides and bottom and begins to
form a rubbery ball (about 20 minutes). The
egg yolks' natural oil prevents it from sticking
to the pan.

TECHNIQUE: In Step 2, if the egg starts to cook too
rapidly, remove from heat immediately and stir
vigorously. This maneuver may have to be repeated
several times to achieve maximum smoothness of the
egg mixture.

When cool enough to handle, form into a cylinder about $9\frac{1}{2}$ inches wide (the width of the bamboo rolling mat). Loosely cover with plastic wrap and cool to room temperature.

Place cooled egg cylinder at the end of sea urchin layer and roll tightly as shown.

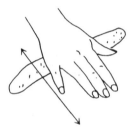

3

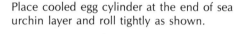

5

4

6

Lay a $9\frac{1}{2}\times10$-inch sheet of plastic wrap on top of bamboo mat (or clean kitchen towel). Arrange sea urchin, in a single layer, smooth side down, to cover surface of plastic wrap.

Place roll, still covered with the wrap and bamboo mat (or towel), in a hot steamer. Steam for 10 minutes at high heat. Remove from steamer and cool to room temperature. Slice and serve.

26 Shrimp Noodles
Ebi Somen

This dish is similar to the French quenelle in that the shrimp is thoroughly pureed and bound with egg. Instead of forming the mixture into the familiar oblong shape, here it is made into noodles. In this case, the noodle is extruded into boiling water from a pastry bag. Japanese kitchen shops sell a tool that extrudes three strands at once, but it is not available in North America.

Shrimp noodles are an excellent addition to clear soup, which is served in a covered lacquer bowl usually at the beginning of a Japanese meal.

<u>TO SERVE FOUR</u>

DIPPING SAUCE:
1 cup noodle-dipping sauce (see page 156)
1 tsp arrowroot

1 lb shrimp
2 tsps salt
1 egg white
1 Tbsp saké
2 quarts *konbu dashi* (see page 156)

GARNISH:
1 scallion, green part only

SPECIAL EQUIPMENT:
food processor
pastry bag

Bring 1 cup noodle-dipping sauce to a boil over medium heat. Add 1 tsp arrowroot that has been mixed with 1 Tbsp water and stir until liquid thickens. Set aside. Shell and devein shrimp.

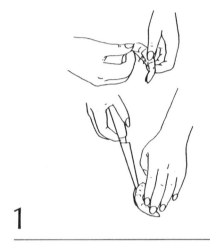

1

2

Place shrimp in a bowl with 1 tsp salt and mix well. Rinse with several changes of cold water. Drain.

Place shrimp in a food processor and puree. Add $\frac{1}{2}$ tsp salt, egg white, saké, and $\frac{1}{4}$ cup *konbu dashi*. Process until very smooth.

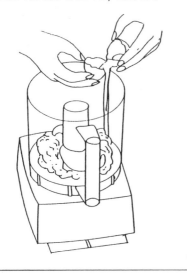

3

Place shrimp mixture into a pastry bag (with a #2 tip) or a mechanical extruding device. Squeeze a long strand into the boiling water. When the noodles float, it is done (about 2 or 3 seconds).

5

4

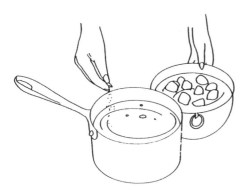

Place remaining *konbu dashi* into a large saucepan with $\frac{1}{2}$ tsp salt and bring to a boil over medium-high heat. Set a large bowl of ice water nearby.

6

Remove immediately, plunge into ice water, and drain. Repeat with the remaining mixture. Refrigerate until serving time. Garnish with slivers of green scallion. Serve noodle-dipping sauce in a sauce boat to be spooned over noodles.

TECHNIQUE: A #2 tip is used in the pastry bag to produce a thin noodle in Step 5. A very smooth shrimp mixture is necessary to pass through this tip, so processing in Step 3 must be thorough. Of course, larger tips may be used, depending on the thickness of the noodle desired.

27 White Island
Kabura-mushi

This turnip dish is a decorative variation of a conventional steamed fish recipe and makes a light, attractive first course.

Beaten egg white is mixed with grated turnip, forming an attractive topping for the fish. A small dot of green *wasabi* paste adds just the right visual and taste accent. Steamed chicken may be substituted for fish if you prefer. Also, eel works well, if you are inclined toward more exotic things.

TO SERVE FOUR

8 oz sea bream (or other white-fleshed fish) fillet
1 tsp saké
$\frac{1}{4}$ tsp salt
12 oz turnips
1 egg white

SAUCE:

$1\frac{1}{3}$ cups *dashi* #1
2 tsps *mirin*
1 tsp sugar
$1\frac{1}{2}$ Tbsps light soy sauce
$1\frac{1}{2}$ tsps arrowroot

2 tsps *wasabi* powder

SPECIAL EQUIPMENT:
clean kitchen towel
steamer

Cut fish fillet into 4 serving portions. Sprinkle fish with salt and saké and set aside in a colander for 10 minutes. Pour 1 quart boiling water over fish. This eliminates fishy taste. Place in individual bowls and set aside.

1

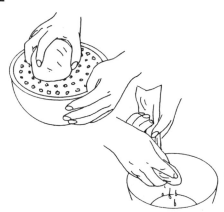

2

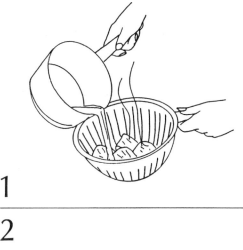

Peel turnips and grate finely. Place in a clean kitchen towel and squeeze the liquid out until pulp is almost dry.

Beat egg white until soft peaks form (do not beat until dry) and add to grated turnip. Mix well.

Combine *dashi*, *mirin*, sugar, and soy sauce in a saucepan and bring to a boil over high heat. Reduce heat so liquid simmers. Add arrowroot mixed with 1 Tbsp water and stir until liquid thickens.

3

5

4

6

Spoon turnip over fish, covering it completely. Place in a heated steamer. Cover and steam for 10 minutes.

Mix *wasabi* powder with 2 tsps water to form a stiff paste. Spoon sauce around the steamed turnip and fish. Dot with a dab of *wasabi* and serve.

28 Steamed Red Snapper
Tai no Domyoji-mushi

In this recipe, the fish is coated with *Domyoji-ko*, which is a granular preparation made from glutinous rice. When steamed, this coating absorbs flavor from the fish, producing a deliciously delicate coating and an interesting texture.

TO SERVE FOUR

12 oz red snapper (or halibut) fillet
1 tsp salt
1 tsp saké
1 cup (approx.) *Domyoji-ko*
4 small pak-choi (or spinach) sprigs
8–12 small fresh *shiitake* mushrooms

BROTH:
1½ cups *dashi* #1
¼ tsp salt
1 Tbsp light soy sauce
3 Tbsps *mirin*

GARNISH:
2 tsps lemon zest cut into needle-thin slivers

SPECIAL EQUIPMENT:
steamer

Slice fish into four serving portions. Sprinkle with salt and saké. Set aside for 10 minutes.

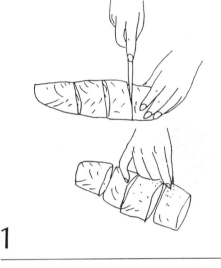

1

2

Bring water to a boil. Have a bowl of ice water ready. Place one piece of fish in a strainer and submerge in boiling water until surface of fish turns opaque, about 30 seconds.

Remove and immediately submerge in ice water. Drain. Repeat with the remaining fish.

Place fish into heated steamer and steam for 5 minutes over medium-high heat. Remove cover and sprinkle each piece of fish with about 2 tsps water. Cover and steam for 5 more minutes.

3

5

4

6

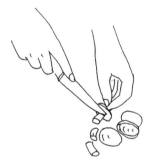

Coat fish thickly with *Domyoji-ko*. Place on plate that will fit into steamer and set aside for 10 minutes before steaming.

Wash *shiitake* mushrooms and cut stems off at the cap.

TECHNIQUE: The secret to the proper preparation of this recipe is in Step 5. After 5 minutes of steaming, the *Domyoji-ko* coating on the fish is moistened with a small amount of water. This provides the necessary moisture to cook the *Domyoji-ko* without oversteaming the fish.

Rinse the pak-choi (or spinach) sprigs. Peel away large outer leaves, using only the tender center of the pak-choi.

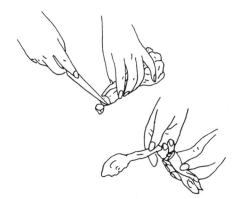

Heat *dashi* and add salt, soy sauce, and *mirin*. Add *shiitake* and cook for 5 minutes over low heat.

7

9

8

10

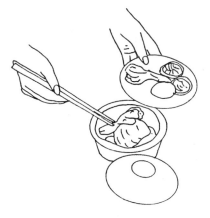

Have a bowl of cold water at hand. Bring 1 quart water to a boil. Add $\frac{1}{2}$ tsp salt and pak-choi. Remove greens immediately and plunge into cold water. Gently squeeze water out and set aside.

Arrange fish, mushrooms, and pak-choi in individual serving bowls. Pour hot broth around the side. Garnish with slivers of lemon zest and serve hot.

29 Tofu Custard with Thick Broth
Kuya-mushi

The Japanese make several varieties of savory custard that can serve as a warming winter soup course. *Chawan-mushi* is perhaps the most well known. Its egg custard conceals bits of chicken, shrimp, mushrooms, and other flavorful morsels.

This dish is a variation that adds a thick broth poured over the custard. It is traditionally served in individual covered china bowls. Such little bowls are available in America now in a full range of prices. You may substitute traditional Western porcelain custard cups, but they do not come with lids, so you miss the fun of the covered presentation.

TO SERVE FOUR

$2 \times 3\frac{1}{2} \times 2$-inch cake regular tofu
4 scallions, white part only
2 eggs
24 ginkgo nuts
4 small fresh *shiitake* mushrooms (or dried, reconstituted), stems removed
4 oz bay scallops
1 cup *dashi* #1
1 Tbsp light soy sauce
1 Tbsp *mirin*
$\frac{1}{2}$ tsp salt

BROTH:

$\frac{2}{3}$ cup *dashi* #1
2 tsps *mirin*
$1\frac{1}{2}$ tsps light soy sauce
$\frac{1}{2}$ tsp salt
2 tsps arrowroot

SPECIAL EQUIPMENT:

weight (1–2 dinner plates)
fine sieve
bowl or *suribachi* (Japanese grinding bowl)
steamer
clean kitchen towel

Wrap tofu in cheesecloth or a clean kitchen towel and place on a slanted cutting board. Weight (with a dinner plate or two) and allow to drain for about 30 minutes. Thread scallions on skewers and grill over open flame. Set aside.

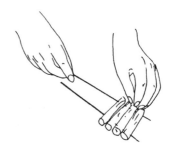

1

2

Beat eggs. Strain tofu and beaten egg through a fine sieve into a bowl (or *suribachi*) then blend in *dashi*, soy sauce, *mirin*, and salt.

Divide scallion, ginkgo nuts, and bay scallops into four portions and put one portion of each into individual serving cups. Save *shiitake* and 8 ginkgo nuts for the broth.

While custard is steaming, combine broth ingredients except arrowroot in a saucepan. Add reserved *shiitake* mushrooms and ginkgo nuts. Bring mixture to a slow boil. Mix arrowroot with 2 tsps water, add a little of the hot broth, and mix well.

3
5
4
6

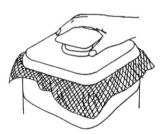

Pour the tofu-egg mixture into the individual cups and place them in a preheated steamer. Cover with clean kitchen towel then with steamer lid. The towel prevents water from dripping onto the surface of the tofu custard. Steam over medium heat until custard sets (about 15 minutes; see TECHNIQUE).

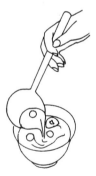

Pour the arrowroot into broth and stir until mixture becomes transparent. Spoon broth into cups of hot custard, making sure that some *shiitake* and ginkgo nuts are in each cup. Serve hot.

TECHNIQUE: The custard is set when a knife inserted in the center comes out clean.

30 Stuffed Winter Melon
Togan no Tsume-mushi

In this recipe, a piece of winter melon is molded around a stuffing of minced *shiitake* mushroom and chicken mixed with egg. It is fun to serve it hidden in a covered bowl. Uncovering the beautiful green sphere is a delightful surprise. A second is in store when the delicious stuffing is discovered concealed within the melon. First courses are a nice opportunity for this kind of playfulness.

TO SERVE FOUR

4 3×3-inch squares of winter melon
2 tsps baking soda
2-inch length of carrot
1 tsp salt

STUFFING:

2 small dried *shiitake* mushrooms
8 oz chicken breast
1 Tbsp oil
2 tsps soy sauce
2 Tbsps saké
1 tsp *mirin*
1 tsp sugar
$\frac{1}{2}$ tsp ginger juice (see page 12)
1 egg

SAUCE:

1 cup *dashi* #1
$\frac{1}{3}$ cup dried bonito flakes (*kezuri-bushi*)
1 Tbsp light soy sauce
1 Tbsp *mirin*
1$\frac{1}{2}$ tsps arrowroot

SPECIAL EQUIPMENT:

cheesecloth
steamer

Remove seeds (and perhaps some flesh) of winter melon, leaving flesh about $\frac{1}{2}$ inch thick. Remove hard skin with vegetable peeler, retaining as much green color as possible.

1

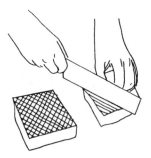

2

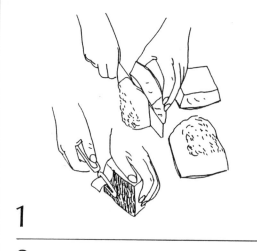

On the skin side, score diagonally with cuts at $\frac{1}{16}$-inch intervals and $\frac{1}{8}$-inch deep. Score again at right angles, forming a grid pattern. Rub $\frac{1}{2}$ tsp baking soda into scored pattern of each piece of melon.

Peel and cut carrot lengthwise into fourths. Slice crosswise into $\frac{1}{8}$-inch slices. Bring 2 cups water to a boil and add 1 tsp salt. Add carrot and cook over medium heat until just tender. Drain and set aside.

To prepare stuffing, soak dried *shiitake* mushrooms in tepid water to cover until reconstituted—about 10 minutes (see TECHNIQUE). Squeeze *shiitake*; filter and reserve soaking liquid. Remove stems and discard. Mince the caps.

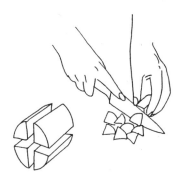

3

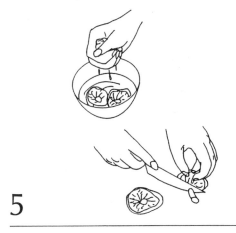

5

4

6

Have a bowl of cold water at hand. Bring 1 quart water to a boil over high heat. Add winter melon pieces, reduce heat to medium, and cook until just tender (about 10 minutes). Remove and place in bowl of cold water to cool.

Skin and bone the chicken breast. Mince very fine with knife or grinder. Heat 1 Tbsp oil in a small saucepan over medium heat. Coat bottom of the pan with oil and pour off excess. Add chicken, mushroom, 2 tsps soy sauce, and the next four ingredients (through ginger juice). Cook, stirring constantly, until the chicken is just done. Beat egg, blend into chicken mixture, and remove from heat.

TECHNIQUE: The time required to reconstitute dried *shiitake* mushrooms will vary greatly depending on their thickness. Ten to 30 minutes seems to be average for mushrooms available in the U.S. Avoid soaking too long, since flavor may be lost. The mushroom is ready when the cap is thoroughly soft and pliable.

Place a piece of winter melon, green side down, on a piece of damp cheesecloth. Remove a little flesh from center and fill with one-fourth of chicken mixture. Bring the corners of the cheesecloth together so that the chicken is wrapped by the melon. While using one hand to form a ball, twist cheesecloth as shown.

7

To make the sauce, heat *dashi* and the liquid in which the mushrooms were soaked in a saucepan over medium heat and add bonito flakes. Simmer until the flakes sink to the bottom. Strain liquid through a paper coffee filter. Do not force it; let it strain slowly if necessary. Return liquid to saucepan and add soy sauce, *mirin*, and reserved carrot slices. Bring to slow boil over medium heat and stir in arrowroot mixed with a little water. Stir until thickened.

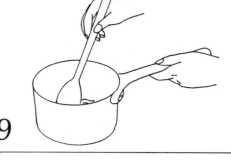

9

8

10

Just before serving, place stuffed melon on a plate and steam in a preheated steamer for about 5 minutes.

Place each hot stuffed winter melon ball in an individual serving bowl. Spoon the sauce over ball and arrange carrot slices attractively (see Plate 30).

31 Tofu Omelet
Gisei Dofu

This omelet recipe mixes tofu with egg for a different omelet taste and texture. A small amount of light soy sauce tints the usual yellow egg color an attractive light tan.

Omelets in Japan are often cut into small rectangular shapes for serving, which allows for a variety of bite-sized arrangements. The omelet is usually cooked in a square or rectangular omelet pan (see Step 6), which eliminates the waste that results with a circular pan. These pans are available in Japanese stores and will make a nice piece of specialty equipment for the "cook who has everything." But a small circular frying pan will also work. The important thing is that the omelet be poured to a thickness of about $\frac{3}{4}$ inch.

TO SERVE FOUR

$2 \times 3 \times 2$-inch cake regular tofu
4 medium dried *shiitake* mushrooms
1 small carrot
10 snow peas
vegetable oil

SEASONING A:

$1\frac{1}{2}$ tsps light soy sauce
1 tsp saké
1 tsp sugar
1 egg

SEASONING B:

2 tsps saké
1 tsp light soy sauce
1 tsp *mirin*

SPECIAL EQUIPMENT:

cheesecloth or clean kitchen towel
weight (1–2 dinner plates)
small frying pan or Japanese omelet pan

Wrap tofu in cheesecloth or a clean kitchen towel and place on a slanted cutting board. Weight (with a dinner plate or two) and allow to drain for about 30 minutes.

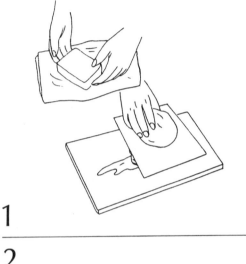

1

2

Soak dried mushrooms in warm water for about 10–30 minutes, depending on thickness, to reconstitute. Squeeze the water from mushrooms and cut off stems. Finely chop mushrooms, carrot, and snow peas and keep them separated.

Heat 1 Tbsp oil in a small saucepan. Add carrot and sauté for 2 minutes. Add mushroom and sauté for another 2 minutes. Add snow peas and seasoning A and sauté until liquid evaporates. Remove from heat and set aside to cool.

Beat egg. Combine all ingredients and Seasoning B in a bowl and mix thoroughly.

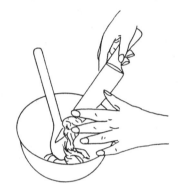

3

5

4

6

Rid tofu of as much remaining water as possible by firmly squeezing it in the cloth. Strain through a fine sieve.

Spread a thin layer of oil in a Japanese omelet (or small frying) pan. When the pan is heated over low heat, pour in the ingredients and cook 7 minutes. Turn and cook other side 5 minutes more. Remove to a plate and allow to cool to room temperature. Slice into rectangles and serve.

32 Walnut "Tofu"
Kurumi Dofu

The tofu variations in Japanese cuisine are endless. There are even variations that don't include tofu at all—but are still called by that name, because the end result resembles it so much.

This dish is an untofu. The tofulike appearance and texture is achieved by grinding blanched walnuts to a paste and thickening this with arrowroot. The solid mixture is cut into clean-edged cubes. A *miso* sauce completes the elegant deception.

<u>TO SERVE FOUR</u>

$\frac{1}{2}$ **cup walnut meats**
$\frac{1}{4}$ **cup arrowroot**
2 cups *dashi* #1

MISO SAUCE:
$\frac{1}{3}$ **cup red *miso***
$\frac{1}{3}$ **cup *mirin***
$\frac{1}{4}$ **cup sugar**

SPECIAL EQUIPMENT:
tofu mold (about 5×5×2 inches) or 1-quart loaf pan
food processor or blender

Blanch walnuts in boiling water for 1 minute. Drain and remove skin from each. This is not as laborious as it sounds and will result in white "tofu" (see Plate 32). If skins are left on, the "tofu" will be tan.

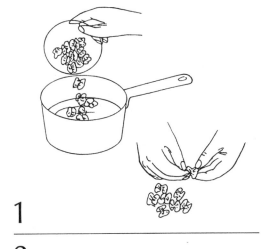

1

2

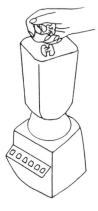

Whir in a food processor or blender to the consistency of peanut butter. A little water may be necessary. Add $\frac{1}{4}$ cup water and whir for 3 minutes more. Blend in arrowroot and *dashi*.

Strain mixture through a sieve into a heavy-bottomed saucepan.

Wet the mold to prevent sticking. Pour in the walnut mixture. Cool, uncovered, at room temperature, then refrigerate for 2 hours.

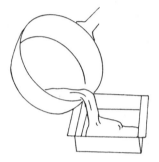

3

5

4

6

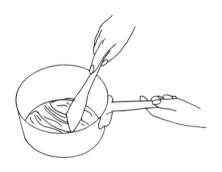

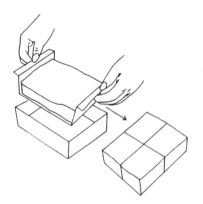

Place the saucepan over low heat and stir with a wooden spatula as it slowly thickens. Scrape the bottom continuously. When you begin to see the bottom of the saucepan between strokes, cook for 1 more minute.

Combine sauce ingredients in a saucepan and cook over low heat, stirring constantly, until sauce reaches the consistency of heavy cream. Demold walnut mixture, slice into sections, place in serving dishes, pour sauce over, and serve.

TECHNIQUE: If the top of the walnut mixture is uneven after molding, it can be steamed slightly and smoothed out with a wet spatula.

33 Tofu with *Miso*
Gion Dofu

G ion is a famous section of Kyoto, which, along with the Pontocho area, was and is the center of that city's geisha world. Exhaustive research, however, has failed to turn up any tales of samurai feasting on this dish while frolicking with geisha. More likely then, the name is simply an acknowledgement that Kyoto is well known for the quality of its tofu.

For this dish the tofu is first pureed and then combined with sesame seeds. It is molded into a bunlike shape with cheesecloth and boiled. At serving it is topped with miso and a spot of hot mustard. The combination of flavors is different and delightful.

TO SERVE FOUR

1½ lbs silk tofu

MISO SAUCE:

⅓ cup red *miso*
⅓ cup sugar
⅓ cup *mirin*
⅓ cup *dashi* #2
1 egg yolk

1 egg white
3 Tbsps white sesame seeds, toasted (see page 13)
2 tsps powdered mustard mixed with enough water to form a stiff paste

SPECIAL EQUIPMENT:
weight (1–2 dinner plates)
food processor or blender
4 8×24-inch pieces of cheesecloth
4 5-inch lengths of string

Wrap tofu in cheesecloth or a clean kitchen towel and place on a slanted cutting board. Weight (with a dinner plate or two) and allow to drain for about 30 minutes. Blend *miso* and sugar in a small saucepan. Slowly add *mirin*, *dashi*, and egg yolk and blend. Cook over low heat, stirring constantly, until the sauce is shiny and thick—about the same consistency as the original *miso*. Remove from the heat and keep sauce warm by placing saucepan in a pot of hot tap water.

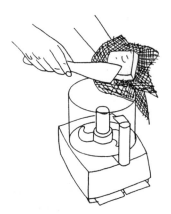

1

2

Bring 2 quarts water to a boil in large saucepan. Puree tofu and egg white in a food processor or blender. Add toasted sesame seeds.

Fold cheesecloth three times to make an
8 × 8-inch square. Place over a small bowl and
pour one-fourth of the tofu puree in the
center.

Place wrapped tofu in boiling water and boil
over medium heat for 12 minutes.

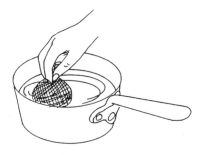

3

5

4

6

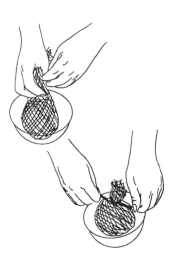

Bring the four corners together and tie with
string.

Remove tofu and drain. Unwrap and invert
onto each serving plate. Spoon warm sauce
over and dot with a dab of hot mustard. Serve
hot.

GRILLED AND
PAN-FRIED DISHES
Yakimono

34 Barbecued Salmon, *Yuan* Style
Sake no Yuan-yaki

The *yuan* style of cooking refers to food marinated in a sauce containing *yuzu*, a citrus fruit with an aromatic skin, which is found in Japan and Korea. The marinade may contain just the rind or several slices if a stronger flavor is desired. Lemon slices here substitute for the unavailable *yuzu*. This marinade can be used for both fish and poultry.

TO SERVE FOUR

1 salmon fillet (about 1 lb)
½ tsp salt

MARINADE:

¼ cup soy sauce
¼ cup saké
¼ cup *mirin*
2 Tbsps sugar
4 lemon slices

GARNISH:
pickled ginger slices

SPECIAL EQUIPMENT:
8 metal skewers
charcoal grill

Cut the salmon into 4 equal pieces. Sprinkle salt on both sides of each fillet and set aside for 15 minutes.

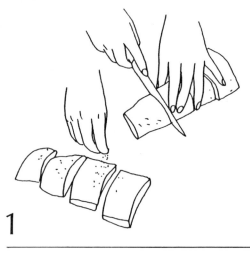

1

2

Combine marinade ingredients in a small saucepan, bring to a boil, and boil for 1 minute over medium-high heat. Pat salmon dry and place in a shallow glass container. Pour cooked marinade over fish. Place slice of lemon on top of each piece and marinate for 1½ hours.

While fish is marinating, start the charcoal. Oil the skewers. Push two skewers in a "fan" angle through each piece of salmon, as shown.

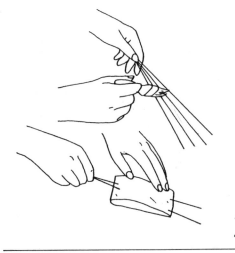

3

4

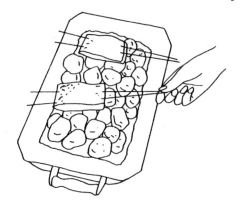

First, begin broiling the meat side, which is going to be on top when served. Broil for 3 minutes. Turn and broil the other side (skin side) for 3 minutes. Brush on marinade several times during broiling.

Serve hot, with a garnish of pickled ginger slices.

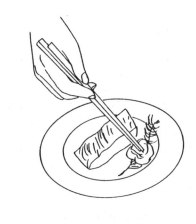

5

35 Chicken-Stuffed *Matsutake* Mushrooms
Matsutake no Hasami-yaki

J ulia Child has been quoted as saying that she likes simple food served simply. She does not like a dish to look as if someone has been fussing with it unnecessarily. Although she was speaking of French food at the time, simple food served simply is the essence of Japanese cuisine.

It is unfortunate that many of the Western chefs who have been looking to Japan for "food decoration ideas" miss this point entirely. The result is ornate, cutesy dishes with which the chef tries to entertain his clientele. The Japanese have long known that the true art of food presentation lies in discarding all nonessentials. In this dish, the delicate pine needle garnish is all that is required for a beautiful presentation.

TO SERVE FOUR

8 oz chicken breast, skinned and boned
3 Tbsps *dashi* #1
1 Tbsp soy sauce
2 tsps *mirin*
2 tsps saké
½ tsp arrowroot

4 medium *matsutake* mushrooms
soy sauce

GARNISH:

pine needles

Rinse pine needles and set aside. Finely chop the chicken and place in bowl. Add *dashi* and mix well.

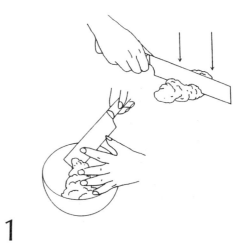

1

2

Combine soy sauce, *mirin*, and saké in a saucepan and add half of the chicken. Cook over low heat, stirring chicken so all lumps separate into crumbles. Cook until just done. Set aside to cool.

Add arrowroot to uncooked portion of chicken. Mix well with a fork and then add cooked chicken.

Preheat oven to broil. Cut mushroom cap in half as shown and stuff with chicken. Brush with soy sauce.

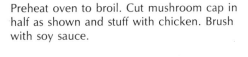

3 **5**

4 **6**

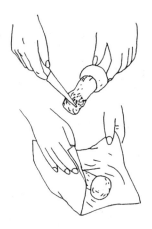

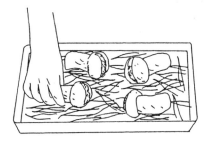

Scrape the bottom of the mushroom stems to rid them of dirt. Rinse under running water. Do not scrape the cap. Pat dry.

Spread the pine needles on a cookie sheet. Place stuffed mushrooms on pine needles and broil for 5–7 minutes, depending on their size. Serve hot, garnished with pine needles.

36 Stones and Moss
Mitsuba no Tori-maki

In sushi, *tekka-maki* refers to red tuna rolled with sushi rice in *nori* seaweed. Although this is a chicken dish and not sushi, it imitates that style of presentation and is quite attractive.

Chicken breast is rolled with trefoil or flat-leafed Italian parsley at its center and lightly fried. The roll is cut into bite-sized pieces and served with grated cucumber.

TO SERVE FOUR

$2\frac{1}{8}$ tsps salt
1 bunch trefoil (about 2 oz) (substitute flat-leafed parsley)
1 whole chicken breast (about 1 lb), skinned and boned
1 Tbsp saké
6-inch length of English cucumber
cornstarch
2 Tbsps vegetable oil

DRESSING:
1 Tbsp rice vinegar
2 Tbsps *mirin*

SPECIAL EQUIPMENT:
wax paper
string

Have a bowl of cold water at hand. Bring 2 quarts of water to a fast boil and add 2 tsps salt. Drop trefoil in and blanch for 10 seconds. Plunge into cold water to stop cooking. Squeeze out water and set aside.

1

2

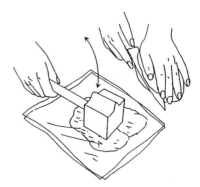

Divide the chicken breast into halves. Butterfly each half by holding the meat flat on the cutting board and slicing parallel to the board lengthwise. Stop the cut about $\frac{1}{2}$ inch before cutting through. Open and flatten between two pieces of wax paper. Pound thoroughly until thin and transparent.

Sprinkle chicken with $\frac{1}{8}$ tsp salt and 1 Tbsp saké. Evenly distribute trefoil on the flattened meat.

Wash cucumber, seed, and grate finely (make about 1 cup). Empty into strainer and set aside to drain. Dust chicken rolls with cornstarch. Heat 2 Tbsps vegetable oil in a large skillet and sauté chicken rolls, shaking pan for even cooking.

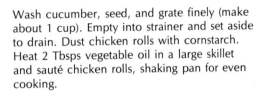

3

5

4

6

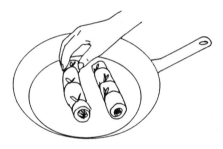

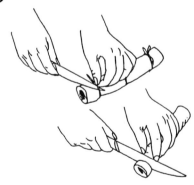

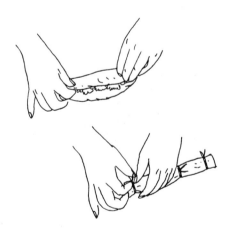

Roll tightly and tie with string in three places. Repeat for remaining chicken.

Cut and remove strings, then cut chicken rolls into 1-inch slices. Arrange attractively on individual serving plates. When ready to serve, mix dressing ingredients with cucumber and spoon over chicken.

37 Broiled Sea Urchin
Yaki Uni

It is said that some cookbook collectors will buy a book just to obtain a single recipe. If that is true, this one is worthy of the honor.

It is a marvelous combination of sea urchin and crab, which has been lightly broiled and sprinkled with poppy seeds. Slicing the molded form into rectangles provides the finishing touch for an elegant hors d'oeuvre or light first course.

TO SERVE FOUR

8 oz cooked crabmeat
1 egg white, lightly beaten
$\frac{1}{4}$ tsp salt
$\frac{1}{2}$ tsp saké
$\frac{1}{2}$ tsp *mirin*
1 container fresh sea urchin roe
$\frac{1}{2}$ egg yolk
black poppy seeds

SPECIAL EQUIPMENT:

2-cup capacity mini-loaf pan
plastic wrap

Shred crabmeat with fingers and add lightly beaten egg white. Add salt, saké, and *mirin* and mix thoroughly with a fork.

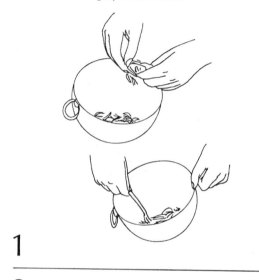

1

2

Pour mixture into 2-cup mini-loaf pan (or similar mold). Cover with plastic wrap and press down to pack tightly. Remove plastic wrap.

TECHNIQUE: Try to use only the body meat (not leg or claw meat) of the crab. Body meat is very white and will make an attractive contrast with the orange-yellow sea urchin.

Gently lay sea urchin roe on top of crab to completely cover.

Place the pan on the broiler rack and broil 6 inches below a preheated broiler unit for 5 minutes. Remove and sprinkle with poppy seeds. When completely cool, slice into approximately $1 \times 2\frac{1}{2}$-inch rectangles. Arrange attractively and serve.

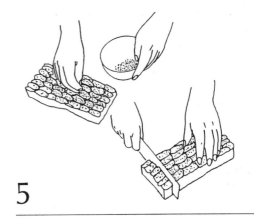

3

5

4

Brush with egg yolk. Repeat brushing several times.

38 Glazed Rainbow Trout
Nijimasu no Uni-yaki

Normally, in a Japanese restaurant this dish would be prepared over charcoal. However, oven cooking produces an equally delicious result. Skewering and constant turning of the delicate fish is not necessary in the oven.

The unusual glaze is made from salted sea urchin roe. Sushi restaurants have introduced many Americans to the slightly sweet, nutty flavored fresh roe of sea urchin. The roe may also be salted and bottled (*neri uni*). The extraordinary glaze here is made by mixing this bottled product with egg yolk, *mirin*, and saké and applying it liberally to the fish during cooking.

TO SERVE FOUR

4 small turnips (1½-inch diameter)
1 Tbsp salt

MARINADE:

2 Tbsps rice vinegar
2 Tbsps *dashi* #1
1½ Tbsps sugar

2 rainbow trout fillets (about 10 inches)
⅛ tsp salt
1 Tbsp saké

GLAZE:

2 Tbsps bottled sea urchin paste (*neri uni*)
1 egg yolk
1 Tbsp *mirin*
1 Tbsp saké

vegetable oil
1 tsp finely grated lemon zest

SPECIAL EQUIPMENT:
disposable chopsticks

(Optional garnish) Peel turnips and trim to uniform spheres. Slice off tops of each to make a flat surface. Place a turnip on its flat surface between two chopsticks, then cut vertically as finely as possible. Chopsticks will prevent knife from cutting through completely. Rotate turnip 90 degrees and repeat cutting. Cut each turnip in the same manner.

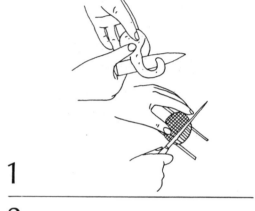

1

2

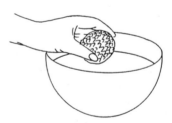

Soak cut turnips in salted water (1 Tbsp salt to 1 quart water) for 10 minutes to soften. Remove and rinse thoroughly. Squeeze out excess water. Mix marinade ingredients in bowl and add turnips. Marinate for 20 minutes or until ready to serve.

Cut each trout fillet in half. Sprinkle $\frac{1}{8}$ tsp salt and 1 Tbsp saké on trout and let sit for 10 minutes.

3

Brush on glaze. Place in the oven and bake for 25 minutes, brushing glaze on at 5-minute intervals. The last brushing should be at 20 minutes. Bake for 5 more minutes. The glaze should not brown.

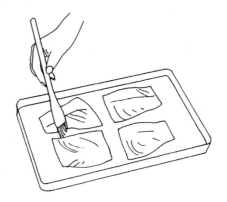

5

4

6

Mix glaze. Heat the oven to 300°F. Lightly oil a cookie sheet and place the fish pieces on it, skin side down.

Place the fish on individual serving plates. Squeeze excess marinade from turnips and sprinkle zest of lemon on each. Serve with fish as edible garnish.

39 Stuffed *Shiitake* Mushrooms
Shiitake no Teri-yaki

When a raw egg yolk is marinated for two or three days in soy sauce and *mirin*, the result is a delicious cheeselike creation. The yolk hardens slightly, becomes a little transparent, and takes on some of the color and flavor of the soy sauce.

The flat round cap of the *shiitake* mushroom serves as the base upon which such a yolk is spread. Salmon roe is served on a companion *shiitake* cap, with equally gratifying results.

As a variation, egg yolks may also be marinated in *miso* for a couple of days. The yolk is simply deposited in a cavity in the *miso*, covered over, and refrigerated. It will take on a distinctive *miso* flavor, which is also excellent for this recipe.

TO SERVE FOUR

MARINATED EGG YOLKS:
¾ **cup soy sauce**
2 **Tbsps** *mirin*
3 **egg yolks**

8 **large fresh** *shiitake* **mushrooms**
1 **Tbsp saké**
2 **Tbsps oil**
¼ **cup salmon roe**

Combine soy sauce and *mirin* in a bowl. Add unbroken egg yolks. Cover with plastic wrap and refrigerate for 2–3 days.

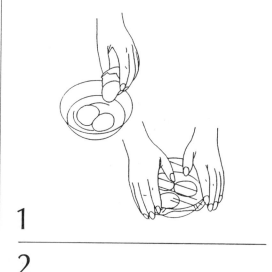

1

2

Cut stems off *shiitake* mushrooms and rinse quickly under running water. Pat dry.

Pour a little saké into each cap. Set aside for 10 minutes.

Spoon salmon roe into underside of 4 *shiitake* caps. Remove egg yolks from marinade and stir into a paste. Spread on underside of remaining *shiitake*.

3

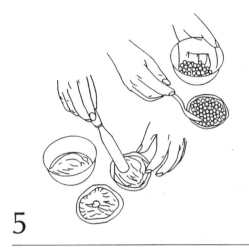

5

4

6

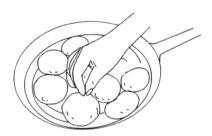

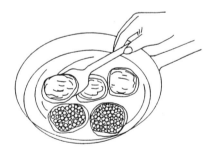

Heat 2 Tbsps oil in a frying pan over medium heat. Add *shiitake* caps, top side up, in a single layer and fry for 1 minute. Remove immediately.

Return stuffed mushroom caps to frying pan with stuffed side up and cook until mushrooms are just done (about 2 minutes). Remove and serve warm.

40 Eggplant with *Miso*
Nasu no Shigi-yaki

For this dish the eggplant should be about 3 inches in diameter. This will yield slices of about the right size for a tasty sample of the fragrant *miso* and creamy eggplant and oil combination without being too filling.

Either red or white *miso* may be used, but white *miso* is sweeter than red, so sugar should be adjusted to taste.

TO SERVE FOUR

SAUCE:
$\frac{1}{4}$ cup white *miso*
1 Tbsp saké
1 Tbsp mirin
1 Tbsp *dashi*
$\frac{1}{2}$ egg yolk
1 tsp finely grated lemon zest
2–3 tsps sugar (optional)

1 eggplant (not more than 3 inches in diameter)
vegetable oil
2 Tbsps saké
2 tsps toasted black sesame seeds

Blend sauce ingredients in small saucepan. Cook over medium-low heat, stirring constantly with wooden spatula until it becomes thick and smooth.

1

2

Cut eggplant into 1-inch-thick slices.

Place large frying pan over low heat and cover bottom with $\frac{1}{8}$ inch oil.

With cover for frying pan ready in your hand, pour the saké in. The oil will spatter, so use the lid as a shield and cover at once. Cook for 3 more minutes.

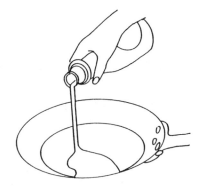

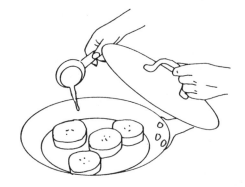

3

5

4

6

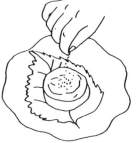

Add eggplant slices and fry for 5 minutes. Turn and fry other side for 3 minutes.

Spread sauce evenly on each hot eggplant slice. Sprinkle on sesame seeds. Serve hot.

41 Pan-Fried Scallops
Hashira no Teri-yaki

When scallops are cooked in Japan, they are flavored with a light sauce, such as the one used here—a mixture of *dashi* #1, soy sauce, and *mirin*, thickened slightly. The lightly fried scallops are presented simply, on individual serving plates. A shell plate was used for the photograph because it relates nicely to the food. The sauce is spooned over, and a bit of fresh grated ginger garnishes the dish. A knot of carrot (softened in lightly salted water for easy tying) is laid across the top.

TO SERVE FOUR

12 large fresh scallops
2 Tbsps saké
2 tsps *mirin*
⅓ tsp salt
½ cup cornstarch
3 Tbsps vegetable oil
**1 thumb-sized piece of fresh ginger root,
    finely grated**

SAUCE:
¾ cup *dashi* #1
2 tsps soy sauce
1 tsp *mirin*
1 tsp arrowroot

Pull off the small, tough section of each scallop and discard. Rinse under cold running water and drain. Combine saké, *mirin*, and salt in a bowl and stir until salt dissolves. Add scallops and marinate 10 minutes.

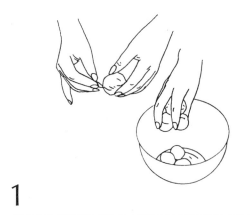

1

2

Finely grate ginger root and set aside.

Combine sauce ingredients in a small saucepan. Bring to a boil over medium heat. Mix cornstarch with 1 Tbsp water, then stir in a little warm sauce. Pour cornstarch mixture into sauce and stir until thickened. Keep warm.

Heat oil in large frying pan over medium heat. Dust excess cornstarch from the scallops and fry for 2 minutes. Turn and fry for 2–3 more minutes. Scallops are done when they feel springy to the touch. Do not overcook.

3 **5**

4 **6**

Dredge scallops with cornstarch.

Serve on individual serving plates with sauce spooned over and a dab of ginger on the side. Scallops are eaten with a touch of ginger.

42 Pinecone Squid
Ika no Matsukasa-yaki

The pinecone effect of this squid preparation is achieved by scoring the meat as shown in Step 5. The key is to undercut the flesh slightly by angling the blade when making the crosshatch cuts. Subsequently, when the squid is broiled over the coals, these flaps curl back, creating the texture.

When broiling, you should allow these flaps to brown slightly. Take care not to overcook the meat, however, or it gets tough.

Although the recipe calls for using the body of the squid only, do not discard the tentacles. They may be cleaned and broiled as well.

TO SERVE FOUR

2 fresh squid (about 8 inches)

MARINADE:
3 Tbsps soy sauce
3 Tbsps *mirin*

GARNISH:
pickled ginger slices

SPECIAL EQUIPMENT:
metal skewers

Gently pull tentacles from squid body.

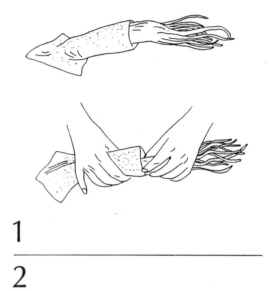

1

2

Cut body open lengthwise.

Cut off head and discard. Clean body thoroughly under running water.

Score the skin side diagonally, starting at one corner. The knife blade should be tilted to undercut the meat a little. Score again at right angles, beginning at the opposite corner.

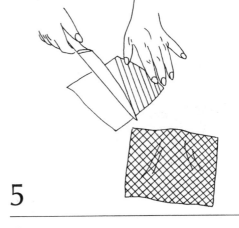

3

5

4

6

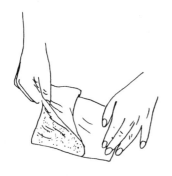

Pull the speckled skin off. If the skin is too slippery, hold squid with a towel.

Mix marinade and marinate for 20–30 minutes.

Thread skewers through the meat as shown.
Do not allow skewers to poke through scored
surface.

Remove skewers with a twisting action and cut
meat into triangles for serving. Garnish with
pickled ginger slices.

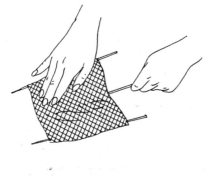

7

9

8

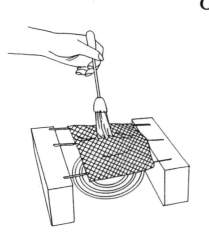

Broil for about 2 minutes or less on each side.
Longer cooking will toughen the meat. Brush
on marinade a couple of times during cooking.

DEEP-FRIED DISHES
Agemono

43 Deep-Fried *Matsutake* Mushrooms
Matsutake no Domyoji-age

The granular *Domyoji-ko* preparation is described on page 155.

Among other things, *Domyoji-ko* is very useful as a coating for fried foods. The rice granules puff up in the hot oil and create an unusually good, crunchy coating, quite unlike any other. One of the dividends of borrowing from an unfamiliar but highly developed cuisine is the new ideas and ingredients that one encounters to make delightful variations on familiar themes.

TO SERVE FOUR

DIPPING SAUCE:

¼ **cup *dashi* #1**
2 Tbsps soy sauce

4 medium *matsutake* mushrooms
flour
1 egg white, lightly beaten
½ cup *Domyoji-ko* (see TECHNIQUE)
vegetable oil for deep-frying

GARNISH:

2 limes

Combine sauce ingredients in a saucepan and bring to a boil. Turn the heat down to low and keep warm.

1

2

Scrape off dirt from bases of *matsutake* stems. Rinse under cold running water. Do not scrub the cap. The outer thin skin of the cap is the source of the highly prized *matsutake* fragrance.

TECHNIQUE: Before using *Domyoji-ko*, dry by spreading on a cookie sheet and placing in a turned-off warm oven for about 10 minutes. Dry *Domyoji-ko* will puff properly.

Pat dry and cut the mushroom into $\frac{1}{3}$-inch-thick slices, as shown.

Gently put two or three mushrooms into the hot oil and fry for a few seconds—just long enough for the *Domyoji-ko* to puff. Remove immediately and drain on a wire rack.

3

5

4

6

Heat oil to 360°F. Dust *matsutake* slices with flour, then dip in egg white and *Domyoji-ko*.

Serve with a garnish of lime halves and dipping sauce on the side. Fried foods are traditionally served on white paper, which acts to absorb oil as well as to insulate food from the cold plate. It is a nice serving touch. Any untreated, good-quality paper may be used if Japanese paper for this purpose is unavailable.

44 Crisp Flounder
Karei no Domyoji-age

Yes, those are fish bones in the photograph. And yes, you're supposed to eat them. After all, why waste perfectly good fish bones—especially if they are delicious when prepared the right way.

The bones of smaller fish and eels are often eaten in this way in Japan. They are first soaked in salted water, hung up to dry, then fried to crunchy perfection. Frequently, a bit more flesh is left on to provide additional texture.

TO SERVE FOUR

2 8-inch flounders (or other flatfish)
3 Tbsps salt

2 Tbsps saké
$\frac{3}{4}$ tsp salt
$\frac{1}{2}$ tsp ginger juice
cornstarch
1 egg white, lightly beaten
***Domyoji-ko* (see TECHNIQUE, page 136)**

vegetable oil for deep-frying

GARNISH:
lemon wedges

Several hours before frying, fillet fish, remove and discard skin, and reserve bones. Refrigerate fillets.

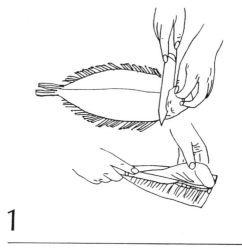

1
_____

2

In a bowl dissolve 3 Tbsps salt in 1 cup water. Soak bones in this solution for 1 hour.

Remove bones and pat dry. Hang bones in cool shade (away from the cat) for several hours until absolutely dry. Curtain hooks are good for this purpose.

Heat oil to 325°F. Fry bones until golden brown and crunchy. Remove and drain. Sprinkle with salt if desired.

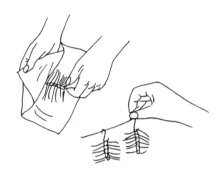

3

5

4

6

Slice each fillet into thirds crosswise. Combine saké, salt, and ginger juice in a small bowl and stir until salt dissolves. Pour this mixture over the fish and marinate for 15 minutes, turning once after about 7–8 minutes.

Pat fillets dry. Dust with cornstarch and shake off excess. Dip in egg white and coat with *Domyoji-ko*. Fry for 2 minutes. Drain on a wire rack, and serve with crisp-fried bones. Garnish with wedges of lemon.

45 Petrale Sole with Bonito Flakes
Shitabirame no Tosa-age

Tosa is the traditional name of the southern portion of Shikoku island. From this area comes the finest bonito. Dried bonito flakes are used to make *dashi*, the all-purpose soup stock of Japanese cuisine.

The *ito-kezuri* bonito shavings used in this recipe are narrower and more threadlike than the bonito flakes used for soup and are often used as garnish atop Japanese greens. In this dish they are used as a coating for deep-frying. The change is delightful, because the bonito imparts its distinctive taste to the mild-flavored sole.

TO SERVE FOUR

1 cup tempura dipping sauce, kept warm (see page 157)
$\frac{1}{2}$ oz *ito-kezuri* dried bonito shavings
$\frac{2}{3}$ cup finely grated daikon radish
2 Tbsps finely grated ginger root
$\frac{3}{4}$ lb petrale sole fillets
cornstarch
1 egg white
1 Tbsp water
vegetable oil for deep-frying

Turn on the oven to warm. Spread *ito-kezuri* bonito shavings on a cookie sheet, place in the oven, and turn off heat immediately. Allow *ito-kezuri* to dry 5 minutes. Remove and set aside.

1

2

Slice the sole into 1 × 2-inch pieces.

Beat egg white with 1 Tbsp water. Heat oil to 360°F. Coat sole pieces with cornstarch and dust off excess. Dip in egg white, coat with *ito-kezuri*, and gently place in hot oil. Fry for about 2 minutes. Drain on a wire rack.

$$\frac{3}{4}$$

Serve with warm tempura sauce and grated daikon and ginger on the side. Add daikon and ginger to the tempura sauce as desired to make a tangy dip for the fish.

46 Scallop *Nori* Rolls
Hashira no Isobe-age

The recipe calls for a mixture of shrimp and scallops to be rolled in *nori* seaweed and deep-fried. The *nori* rolls are then sliced into bite-sized pieces to make attractive hors d'oeuvres.

Care should be taken not to overheat the oil. *Nori* burns quite easily, so special attention is needed during the frying.

TO SERVE FOUR

1 cup tempura dipping sauce, kept warm (see page 157)
6 oz shrimp
1 tsp salt
8 oz scallops
1 egg
1 egg yolk
1 tsp *mirin*
1¼ tsps salt
20 5-inch stems trefoil or flat-leafed parsley (optional)
2 sheets *nori* seaweed
cornstarch
vegetable oil for deep-frying

GARNISH:
fried ginkgo nuts (optional)

SPECIAL EQUIPMENT:
bamboo rolling mat (*makisu*) or clean kitchen towel

Shell and devein shrimp. Add 1 tsp salt and mix with fingers. Rinse with cold water. Smash shrimp well under flat surface of knife blade, then chop finely to a pastelike consistency.

1

2

Clean scallops. Pull off small tough section of each scallop and discard. Shred with fingers. Add to shrimp.

Beat egg and egg yolk well. Pour through sieve into top of double boiler. Add *mirin* and salt. Cook over simmering water while stirring with a wooden spatula until the mixture reaches the thickness of mayonnaise. Remove from heat and blend in shrimp and scallop mixture.

Heat oil to 300°F. Place one-half sheet *nori* on a bamboo rolling mat (or clean kitchen towel). Spread one-fourth of seafood mixture and one-fourth of parsley stems onto the *nori*. Leave the $\frac{1}{2}$ inch of *nori* farthest from you uncovered.

3

5

4

6

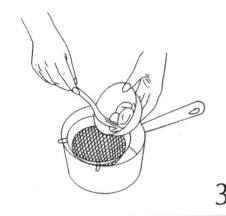

Blanch trefoil or parsley stems. Cut each sheet of *nori* in half crosswise.

Roll up. The moisture from the seafood mixture will seal the *nori* cylinder. Lightly dust the ends with cornstarch. Fry at 325°F for $1\frac{1}{2}$ to 2 minutes. Remove and drain on a rack. Cut into 1-inch slices and serve with tempura dipping sauce on the side for dipping. A few ginkgo nuts may be fried in the oil to garnish if you like.

47 Prawn Fantasy
Ebi no Mino-age

This dish is similar to tempura, but the prawns are not fried in butter. Instead a "cocoon" is made of julienned potatoes tied together with strips of gourd ribbon. The result is a lighter, more delicate dish.

TO SERVE FOUR

2 large boiling potatoes
16 4-inch strips of gourd ribbon (*kampyo*)
8 prawns
3 Tbsps saké
½ tsp salt
vegetable oil for deep-frying
1 egg white
1 Tbsp water
flour
cornstarch

GARNISH:

lemon slices

Peel and julienne potatoes. Soak in 1 quart water for 30 minutes. Soak gourd ribbon in water for 20 minutes.

1

2

Shell prawns, leaving the tail and the last section of shell intact. Cut tails off as shown (see TECHNIQUE). Devein prawns.

TECHNIQUE: Japanese chefs cut the tails of prawns before frying as shown. The center, pointed section of the tail is hollow and contains water. Cutting drains this cavity and thus prevents serious spattering in the hot oil.

Score underside of prawns at $\frac{1}{4}$-inch intervals. This prevents prawns from curling when fried. Combine saké and salt in a bowl and marinate prawns for 5 minutes.

Place two parallel gourd ribbon lengths on a plate. On this lay one-eighth of julienned potato as shown. Coat each prawn with flour, dip in egg white, and coat with cornstarch.

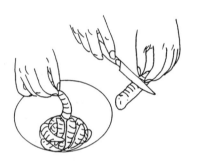

3

5

4

6

Heat oil to 360°F. Beat egg white with water. Drain potato and gourd ribbon and pat dry. Place potato on large plate and sprinkle with 3 Tbsps cornstarch. Mix well.

Place prawn on potatoes and cover with potato pieces. Tie with gourd ribbon as shown. Deep-fry in oil at 360°F for about 3 minutes. Adjust heat so potato does not burn. Garnish with standing half-slices of lemon (see Plate 47).

48 Spring Rain Tempura
Masu no Harusame-age

*H*arusame is made from potato starch or soybean powder with gelatin. The filaments are extruded and cut. *Harusame* literally translated means "spring rain." These filaments are sometimes softened with water and formed into a bed of white, translucent strands upon which vegetables or seafood are served. In this recipe, pieces of trout are coated with dry *harusame* and then quickly deep-fried to create a tasty, decorative variation of the traditional tempura coating.

TO SERVE FOUR

1 cup tempura dipping sauce, kept warm (see page 157)
4 trout fillets
1 Tbsp saké
$\frac{1}{2}$ tsp salt
$\frac{1}{4}$ tsp white pepper
1 egg white
1 Tbsp water
3 oz *harusame*
vegetable oil for deep-frying

Cut each fillet of trout crosswise into three pieces. Place fish on a plate and sprinkle with saké, salt, and pepper. Set aside for 15 minutes.

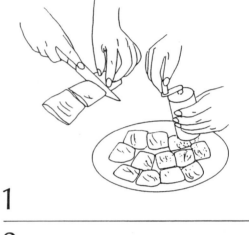

1

2

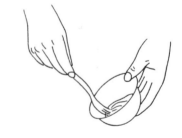

Beat egg white with 1 Tbsp water.

Cut *harusame* into $\frac{1}{2}$-inch lengths.

Gently place in hot oil. The *harusame* will puff up immediately. Turn once and fry for about 30 seconds. Remove immediately and drain on a wire rack. Serve three pieces of fish in each individual serving dish. Add tempura sauce as a dip in individual bowls. Fry snow peas as a garnish, or, if you prefer, serve with pickled ginger slices.

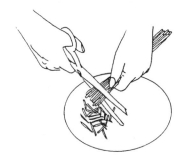

3

5

4

Heat oil to 360°F. Dip the fish in egg white and then coat with *harusame*.

49 Shrimp in Noodle Basket
Ebi no Tsuto-age

In old Japan and in many countries before the age of cheap plastics, straw and other natural materials were used for packaging.

This dish evokes those old packaging methods. Of course, in this case, the "straw" is edible *somen* noodles, which contain a light shrimp and egg mixture.

TO SERVE FOUR

1 cup tempura dipping sauce, kept warm (page 157)
8 5-inch lengths of gourd ribbon (*kampyo*)
12 oz dried *somen* noodles
6 shrimp
2 string beans
3 eggs
3 cups *dashi* #2
$\frac{1}{4}$ tsp salt
1 Tbsp *mirin*
vegetable oil for deep-frying

GARNISH:

8 small mild green peppers or strips of bell pepper

SPECIAL EQUIPMENT:

8 8-inch squares cheesecloth
steamer

Soak gourd ribbon lengths in warm water for 20 minutes.

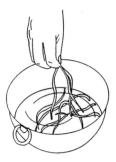

1

2

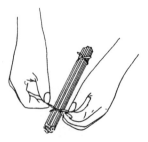

Cut *somen* noodles into 6-inch lengths and divide into 4 equal bundles. Pat dry gourd ribbon and tie each bundle of *somen* noodles at both ends as shown. Set aside.

Shell and devein shrimp. Rinse and cut into $\frac{1}{2}$-inch pieces. Chop string beans into $\frac{1}{4}$-inch pieces. Beat eggs and shrimp and string bean.

Pour one-fourth of egg mixture directly into the hot *dashi*. Poach until almost done. Pour poached egg and *dashi* into the cheesecloth-lined strainer. Reserve *dashi* that collects in bowl beneath strainer to be used again.

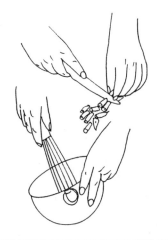

3

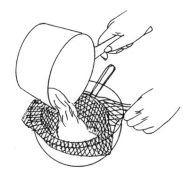

5

4

6

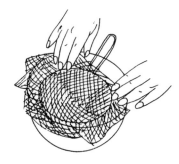

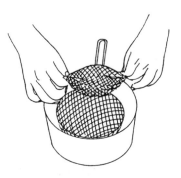

Bring *dashi* to a boil and add salt and *mirin*. Reduce heat to medium-low. Dampen cheesecloth and place a double layer in a medium-sized strainer over a bowl as shown.

Gather each end of the cheesecloth and form poached egg into an oval shape, squeezing out excess *dashi*. Set aside in cheesecloth until cool. Pour collected *dashi* back into saucepan and reheat. Repeat Steps 5 and 6 three more times.

Place *somen* bundles in a heated steamer and steam until they are pliable.

Deep-fry bundles in 350°F oil until noodles are the color of straw. Serve with warm tempura dipping sauce, to be poured into individual bowls. Garnish with lightly fried, small, mild green peppers or strips of bell pepper for a nice color contrast. Chopsticks are a better implement for managing the crispy fried noodles than a knife and fork.

7

9

8

Place one-fourth of cooked egg mixture in each bundle (see Plate 49).

ASPICS
Nikogori

50 Whitebait in Aspic
Shirauo-kan

This recipe uses whitebait in an agar-agar aspic lightly flavored with soy sauce, saké, and *dashi*. The linear white pattern of the fish shows through the translucent aspic, creating an attractive composition that works splendidly as a first course or hors d'oeuvre.

TO SERVE FOUR

½ bar agar-agar (*kanten*)
½ lb whitebait (shrimp may substitute)
1 cup *dashi* #1
1 tsp saké
2 Tbsps light soy sauce

GARNISH:

daikon sprouts

SPECIAL EQUIPMENT:

tofu mold or 2-cup capacity mini-loaf pan

Tear agar-agar into small pieces and soak in water to cover for 2 hours.

1

2

Rinse whitebait in cold water and soak in salted water (1 Tbsp salt in 1 quart water) for 5 minutes. Drain fish and lay in a single layer on a small plate.

Place plate with whitebait in a preheated steamer. Steam for 2 minutes over medium heat. Repeat until all fish are cooked. Cut off heads and tails.

Pour agar-agar mixture into tofu mold or 2-cup loaf pan. Place whitebait in the mixture, cool to room temperature, then refrigerate.

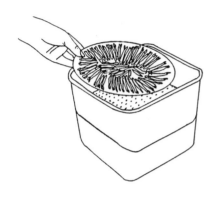

3

5

4

6

Squeeze water out of agar-agar and place in a saucepan. Place *dashi*, saké, and soy sauce in saucepan, then add agar-agar. Cook over low heat until agar-agar dissolves.

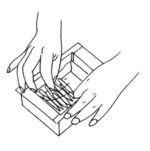

When aspic sets, slice and serve.

Sauces and Dressings

DASHI

Dashi is the basic soup stock for Japanese cuisine. Instant *dashi* is available in powdered, granular, tea bag, and concentrated liquid forms. These are frequently used, but cannot compare to a well-made fresh *dashi*. The powdered and granular forms contain MSG and salt, which some may prefer to avoid. Remember to compensate for this added salt if these preparations are used. Thin chicken stock is sometimes used as a substitute in American kitchens—but this is only a last resort compromise.

Dashi has no strict rules for its preparation. Japanese chefs all have their own secrets and variations much like their European counterparts have for the preparation of chicken or beef stocks. What follows is simply one version of this hard-working stock.

Dashi has two variations for slightly different uses.

Dashi #1

6 × 6-inch piece *konbu* kelp
2 cups dried bonito flakes

• 1. Wipe *konbu* kelp clean with a damp cloth. Do not wash it, because you will lose much of the flavor.
• 2. Place *konbu* in a saucepan with 5 cups water over medium heat. Just before the water comes to a boil, remove *konbu*. If you cook it, the *konbu* develops a strong odor. Save the *konbu* for *dashi* #2.
• 3. Add the bonito flakes and skim off foam. Turn the heat off immediately. When the flakes settle to the bottom of the saucepan, strain the stock through a fine silk sieve or coffee filter. Do not squeeze. Reserve bonito flakes for *dashi* #2.
• 4. *Dashi* #1 is used for clear soup and as a base for sauces.

Dashi #2

• 1. Combine 5 cups water and the reserved *konbu* and bonito flakes. Add a small handful of dried bonito flakes. Bring to a boil over medium heat. Strain liquid through cheesecloth and discard bonito flakes and *konbu*. Simmer for 5 minutes over low heat. Strain again.
• 2. Whereas *dashi* #1 is used for delicate clear broths, etc., *dashi* #2 is for more strongly flavored foods such as *miso* soup, fish, and meat dishes, etc.

DOMYOJI-KO

Domyoji-ko is glutinous rice that has been steamed, dried, and granulated. The name comes from the fact that it was originally prepared at the Domyoji temple in Osaka as a preserved food for times of famine. The suffix *-ko* means "powder."

In the event that packaged *Domyoji-ko* is not available, it may be made as follows:

• 1. Wash 2 cups of glutinous rice and soak in 5 cups water overnight. Drain.
• 2. Line the top of a steamer with cheesecloth.
• 3. Place the drained rice on the cheesecloth to a thickness of not more than $1\frac{1}{2}$ inches.
• 4. Steam over high heat for 20 minutes.
• 5. Lift the lid and sprinkle water over the rice with your hand. Cover and steam for 5 more minutes. Repeat 3 or 4 times. Use about $\frac{3}{4}$ cup of water total.
• 6. Remove the rice from the steamer and spread out on a large basketry tray (or cookie sheet). Dry thoroughly.
• 7. Whir $\frac{1}{4}$ cup at a time in a blender until the rice grains are cut into fourths, approximately.

NOTE: If *Domyoji-ko* is to be used for deep-frying, be sure that it is completely dry by placing it in a turned-off warm oven for about 30 minutes. Use this procedure even for the packaged variety. This will insure that the grains puff properly.

FLAVOR VINEGAR (Sanbai-zu)

Flavor vinegar (sanbai-zu) is similar to vinegar-soy sauce except that a little less soy sauce is used and salt and sugar are added. It is good for salads such as cucumber, fish, or shellfish. Mix the following:

3 Tbsps rice vinegar
2 tsps light soy sauce
2 Tbsps dashi #1
$\frac{1}{2}$ tsp salt
2 tsps sugar

KONBU DASHI

Many varieties of konbu kelp are eaten in Japan. The best konbu for dashi is said to be makonbu variety, which is harvested off the coast of Hakodate in Hokkaido. It grows to seven feet in length and perhaps a foot wide with very thick flesh. This konbu has such a fine fragrance and flavor that it is also powdered and used to make a delicate konbu tea (konbu-cha).

Konbu dashi is a vegetarian dashi (without bonito flakes). It is made by simply soaking konbu in water.

When choosing konbu, avoid kelp that is excessively black, since that indicates the konbu is too mature. A blackish green color is preferable. Store konbu in a cool dry place.

• 1. Clean a 6 × 12-inch piece of konbu by wiping with a damp cloth. Do not wash.
• 2. Soak in 5 cups water for about 2 hours at room temperature. Discard the konbu.

LEMON-SOY SAUCE (Ponzu-joyu)

This sauce is distinctive because of its use of citrus, which gives a light, tart quality. It is good for fish, chicken, oysters, prawns, etc. If you happen to be growing Meyer lemons in your garden, use them. They are milder and close to the Japanese citron called yuzu.

If tamari is not available, add another Tbsp of soy sauce.

$\frac{1}{4}$ cup lemon juice
$\frac{1}{4}$ cup soy sauce
1 Tbsp tamari

NOODLE-DIPPING SAUCE (Tsuke-zuyu)

This is the traditional dipping sauce for noodles.

2 cups dashi #2
$\frac{1}{4}$ cup light soy sauce
$\frac{1}{4}$ cup mirin
2 cups dried bonito flakes

• 1. Combine ingredients in a saucepan and bring to a boil over medium heat.
• 2. Reduce heat and simmer for 10 minutes. Strain through a fine sieve or coffee filter.

PLUM VINEGAR (Uma-zu)

Plum vinegar is considered to be the tastiest of all Japanese sauces. It is used primarily with shellfish. One of its ingredients, pickled plums (umeboshi), is enjoying much attention again in Japan today because of its reputed healthful properties.

2 pickled plums (umeboshi)
2 inch-length konbu kelp
1/2 cup saké
3/4 cup mirin
2 ounces dried bonito flakes
1/4 cup rice vinegar (or to taste)
1/2 tsp light soy sauce
salt to taste

• 1. Soak the pickled plums in 1 cup water overnight. Drain. Remove and discard seeds.
• 2. Combine plum flesh, konbu kelp, saké, and mirin in a saucepan and cook over low heat until reduced to about 70 percent of its original volume.
• 3. Add dried bonito flakes, soy sauce, and vinegar. Remove from heat.
• 4. Strain through a fine sieve.

SWEET VINEGAR (Ama-zu)

This is a sauce for mild-flavored fish or shellfish. It is somewhat sweeter than other Japanese vinegar sauces. Simply mix and serve.

$\frac{1}{2}$ cup rice vinegar
$\frac{1}{2}$ cup dashi #1
$\frac{1}{4}$ cup sugar
small pinch salt or jot of soy sauce

TEMPURA DIPPING SAUCE

This dipping sauce is for deep-fried fish and vegetables and it is served warm if you like it sweeter. Add a little sugar.

½ cup *mirin*
2 cups *dashi* #1
½ cup soy sauce

● 1. Warm the *mirin* in a saucepan and ignite with a match. Rotate the pan slowly until the alcohol burns off.
● 2. Add the remaining ingredients.

TOSA SOY SAUCE (*Tosa-joyu*)

Tosa soy sauce is flavored with dried bonito flakes, *mirin*, and saké. It is marvelous with sashimi.

1 cup soy sauce
1½ Tbsps *mirin*
½ Tbsp saké
1½ cups dried bonito flakes

● 1. Combine ingredients in a saucepan and bring to a boil over medium heat.
● 2. Boil until volume is reduced by 10 percent. Remove from heat and strain into a clean jar with an airtight cover. Refrigerate. Tosa soy sauce will keep for about two weeks.

TOSA VINEGAR (*Tosa-zu*)

Tosa vinegar is a variation of vinegar-soy sauce (*nihai-zu*) and flavor vinegar (*sanbai-zu*). It is enhanced by the addition of dried bonito flakes. It is excellent as a dipping sauce with white-fleshed fish, squid, octopus, and shellfish.

¾ cup vinegar-soy sauce or flavor vinegar
½ cup dried bonito flakes

● 1. Bring the vinegar-soy sauce to a boil over medium-low heat in a saucepan.
● 2. Add the bonito flakes and bring back to a boil. When the vinegar smell subsides, remove from heat and strain.

VINEGAR-SOY SAUCE (*Nihai-zu*)

Vinegar-soy sauce (*nihai-zu*) is especially well suited as a dressing or dipping sauce for raw fish and raw shellfish. Mix the following:

3 Tbsps rice vinegar
1 Tbsp light soy sauce
2 Tbsps *dashi* #1

Index